D1600415

Torrens in the United States

Torrens in the United States

**A Legal and Economic History and Analysis
of American Land-Registration Systems**

Blair C. Shick
Irving H. Plotkin
Arthur D. Little, Inc.

Lexington Books
D.C. Heath and Company
Lexington, Massachusetts
Toronto

51370

Library of Congress Cataloging in Publication Data

Shick, Blair C
    Torrens in the United States.

    Bibliography: p.
    Includes index.
    1. Torrens system—United States. 2. Land titles—Registration and transfer—United States. 3. Torrens system—Economic aspects—United States. 4. Land titles—Registration and transfer—Economic aspects—United States. I. Plotkin, Irving H., joint author. II. Title.
KF679.S5   346'.73'0438   78-13810
ISBN 0-669-02666-2

Published simultaneously in Canada.

Printed in the United States of America.

International Standard Book Number: 0-669-02666-2

Library of Congress Catalog Card Number: 78-13810

Contents

List of Figures and Tables

Acknowledgments

The subject matter of this book proved particularly challenging because of the breadth and mix of disciplines required to gather and analyze pertinent information. Land ownership and development is so central to the infrastructure of a functioning society as to require a vast array of perspectives and insights for thorough understanding. We are indebted to literally dozens of practicing lawyers, judges, mortgage officers, surveyors, title examiners, land-registration administrators, and others who freely contributed their time and experience. Special appreciation is extended to Judge William Randall of the Massachusetts Land Court and to Richard Edblom, Esq., and John LoSasso, Esq., the respective chief examiners for the Hennepin County (Minnesota) and Cook County (Illinois) Torrens offices. Our overall assessment of the appropriateness of land registration for modern America is not a positive one. But our criticism lies with the conceptual underpinnings of the registration approach and the excessive (even panacea-like) expectations sometimes placed upon it, not with the special services provided by the programs administered by these professionals.

Support for our efforts came from several sources. This study was originally undertaken with the assistance of the American Land Title Association. Arthur D. Little, Inc., and our numerous colleagues there extended the additional resources and support needed to prepare the study for formal publication. To single out one or more contributors for thanks risks unfairness to those excluded; but some mention must be made of special contributions. Ann Venable performed the indispensable task of shaping an unwieldy manuscript into manageable form, while Mary Ahearn reviewed the entire text. Anne Flaherty and Barbara Frankel carried the burden of typing numerous revisions. Our wives and families paid the incalculable costs of our seemingly interminable preoccupation.

Finally, there are the friends neighbors, and colleagues who own or have owned registered land and who thought our questions would never stop. Thank you, all.

Cambridge, Massachusetts
August 1978

Blair C. Shick
Irving H. Plotkin

Summary

Purpose and Scope

This book examines the United States experience with Torrens—or land-registration—systems. Under Torrens, ownership interests in real property are established and transferred pursuant to a governmental certification and registration process. The process also requires, for possible legal enforceability, the recording (on a master ownership certificate maintained by a public office) of certain nonownership interests that exist, or are claimed to exist, in the property.

The fundamental distinction between Torrens and conventional real-property legal mechanisms lies in the scope of the government's responsibility with respect to establishing and transferring ownership, and not in differences in techniques for recording and storing information appropriate thereto. In the conventional approach, the government's role is limited to providing recording and indexing systems for storage and retrieval of documents evidencing claims to ownership and other interests. However, the validity of all interests (including ownership) is established and effected through private legal efforts and relationships and is not "certified" by the government.

Each of the fifty states has a land-records or deed-recording system. In fact, the recording of deeds in a public office is an American innovation, reportedly first established in the Plymouth colony about 1624. Although this system spread to the other North American colonies, it was not generally developed in England or in other British territories. It is probable that this lack of a public land-records system provided the major impetus for the developments that led to experimentation with Torrens in many English-speaking jurisdictions, beginning with Australia in 1858. Nevertheless, toward the end of the nineteenth century, several American states authorized the use of land registration. Only a handful of the many systems that were started have survived with any degree of viability.

Focusing primarily, but not exclusively, on the four major surviving urban systems, this study sought to understand how Torrens actually works in American applications. The study evaluates the real-world effectiveness, strengths, and weaknesses of the Torrens operation. An underlying concern was whether replacing or supplementing the conventional real-property system with the Torrens approach offers a realistic possibility of achieving social and private savings in residential real-estate closing costs. Thus, in large part, our study was aimed at a cost/benefit analysis of Torrens, especially from the perspective of the homeowner and taxpayer. However, important qualitative and legal considerations also were observed and reported.

In addition to examining in close detail the most important survivors of the numerous American experiments with the Torrens system, we reviewed the scholarly and practical literature, both here and abroad, about land registration. Our findings and conclusions are based on direct observations of the working of the major Torrens systems in the United States, on numerous personal interviews with system administrators and users (lenders, attorneys, insurers, and others), on review of system financial reports and charges, on the reactions of local experts to our initial analysis of the studied systems, and on the available literature.

Our emphasis on observing actual Torrens operations is based on our belief that only in the real world can one obtain the information necessary to evaluate any specific proposed Torrens operations or the concept in general. While the literature abounds with theoretical and legalistic discussions of the Torrens approach (and much justified criticism of the conventional real-property system), there is very little contemporary discussion of Torrens' economics and practicability based upon actual observation. Our goal was to fill this important and critical void, thereby contributing an empirical basis to the discussion of the relative merits of systems for controlling and reducing residential closing costs.

Observations and Findings

1. The Torrens concept has not found widespread acceptance in the United States:

a. Torrens was authorized in twenty-one states, of which twenty actually enacted enabling legislation, mainly during the period between 1895 and 1915. Six states subsequently repealed the legislation. Nine others used Torrens only infrequently, and even this limited use ceased before the Great Depression. Ohio has a few active urban systems that survived into the post-World War II era, but these have experienced substantial declines in usage. This leaves only four states with significant current experience with Torrens: Massachusetts, Hawaii (with a system modeled on that used in Massachusetts), Illinois (in Cook County only), and Minnesota.

b. Voluntary landowner use of Torrens in the United States has been limited almost entirely to urban areas and for purposes associated with the elimination of historical title defects. Despite the number of rural states that enacted Torrens legislation, the actual incidence of use in rural areas was infrequent at best.

c. Historically, Torrens received its heaviest use as a facilitator of rapid urban growth involving land being developed for the first time that was the subject of unclear title histories or boundaries (for example, in the metropolitan Boston area) or that lacked provable records (for example, in Cook County, Illinois, where the public records were destroyed in 1871 by the Chicago fire).

2. Land registration under Torrens was and is sought for reasons specific to the property in question. The most prevalent and important reasons that have continued over time include the following:

a. Where conventional judicial methods for quieting title are inadequate, land registration is sought to cure unmarketable titles; that is, to resolve doubts or conflicts about title—resulting from ambiguities, gaps, and other current and historical defects—that prevent the sale of land. This has been and continues to be the primary use of Torrens in the United States.

b. In Massachusetts, and occasionally elsewhere, registration is used for the establishment and clarification of precise boundary lines.

c. Torrens certification precludes the establishment of an interest in land, by possession or prescriptive use, that is adverse to the interest of the registered owner.

d. The developer of a large industrial or commercial complex involving multiple parcels of land may occasionally seek to register the complex in order to obtain a unified title, recorded in a single certificate for the integrated parcel.

e. In the systems studied, land cannot be withdrawn from its Torrens status once the initial registration decree is entered. As a result, most of the land that is currently registered, including well over a majority of the homeowner properties involved, continues to be registered because of the actions of prior owners. New owners have no choice but to accept the registration system.

3. Many of the needs of landowners met by Torrens have been almost eliminated or have declined in importance over the years as the amount of urban land subject to significant disputes or lacking recorded title history has diminished. The number of new land registrations has declined substantially in the jurisdictions studied and has almost ceased in one.

4. In the absence of compelling special circumstances relating to title or boundary defects, individual homeowners rarely seek to have their property registered.

5. Our study of the literature reveals that the Torrens system is often perceived as a way of correcting deficiencies in current real-property information mechanisms. For example, the mandatory recording on the Torrens certificate of various outstanding interests in a specific land parcel is viewed as a substantial improvement in record keeping. However, tract indexes such as those already in use by many deed-recording offices achieve the identical function without the cumbersome legal and administrative trappings of Torrens. Similarly, automation of land records is occurring without Torrens. Other reforms for which Torrens has been proposed have been achieved directly in many states by such substantive legislation as marketable title acts and curative title acts.

6.   Because of exceptions established by the enabling legislation, by judicial decisions, by other statutory provisions, and by the nature of our federal/ state system, the Torrens certification of ownership is not conclusive as to all claims or interests that might exist in a given land parcel. Some of the more significant claims or interests that may override the Torrens certification are as follows:

a.   Claims or interests based on federal law or the U.S. Constitution, including federal tax liens, claims and interests arising from bankruptcy proceedings, and claims by Indian tribes, such as those that have been brought recently under the Non-intercourse Act of 1790.

b.   Claims or interests arising from appellate processes pertaining to the initial registration decree, including the right to appellate review for persons who were not a party to the registration proceeding.

c.   Interests arising from current local and municipal taxes and special assessments.

d.   Possessory interests of persons occupying property under leases of up to seven years.

e.   Mechanic's liens (claims for payment for materials or work to improve land) during the period between the time the work is performed or the materials supplied and the time the claim is required to be filed.

7.   The Torrens certificate does not assure or determine the priority among liens or other nonownership interests in land. While the registration process provides a mortgage lender with limited protection against some interests not appearing on the certificate, it does not fulfill the lender's need to secure priority against all possible interests in the property other than that of the owner.

8. Torrens does not protect lenders and others from risks such as those arising from mishaps or failures in a current transaction or from external sources (for example, adverse legal decisions on usury or permissive land use). Risks such as these are not related to title *per se* but may affect the utility or enforceability (and hence marketability) of interests in land.

9.   Because of these different legal limitations on Torrens certification, registration of land in a Torrens system alone does not assure a potential buyer of peaceful and exclusive enjoyment of his or her purchase nor does it provide a potential lender with a legal basis regarded as sufficient for a prudent investment decision. Further, the full import of either the presence or absence of entries on the Torrens certificate is not self-explanatory, even to an attorney specializing in real estate. As a result, buyers of and investors in registered property seek a level of professional assistance for title search, examination, and insurance that is comparable to the assistance sought for unregistered land.

10.   Title insurance is purchased for registered as well as unregistered land consistent with the customs and practices that prevail in the different areas with

Torrens systems. For the reasons discussed earlier, mortgage lenders and others seeking title insurance generally make few exceptions to their insurance requirements when the land involved is registered.

11. The owner of registered property incurs certain risks and cost requirements because the validity of the ownership interest, together with the existence of certain other claims and interests, is determined by the Torrens certificate, which is in the possession of a public office. These risks include the following:

a. Torrens reverses a fundamental jurisprudential concept of American land ownership. If an innocent purchaser buys registered land from one claiming to be the person shown on the Torrens certificate as owner, although such land was conveyed by forgery, the loss is borne by the defrauded owner rather than the purchaser. Under the law applicable to the conventional real-property system, a forgery cannot convey title, so the loss is borne by the purchaser.

b. Erroneous information can be entered on the Torrens certificate by administrative error without the owner's knowledge. The error so entered has legal force until it is removed. The removal process may require court action, with the owner bearing related legal costs.

c. Changes in ownership circumstances that are not related to an actual transfer of ownership between different parties (for example, because of a divorce or because of the death of a registered owner) require special proceedings to change the official certificate to conform to the the new ownership status. These and other proceedings necessitated by the dominant role of the Torrens certificate require additional legal and administrative (filing) expenses.

12. The public insurance funds established for Torrens systems are available only to compensate for damages sustained as a result of administration of the system. The funds are not available for losses occasioned by mishaps or failures in the transaction giving rise to a transfer of registered land. Further, the funds are small and the extent of losses covered is circumscribed and uncertain. For example:

a. In the urban systems studied, only one fund exceeds $400,000. The experience is that few claims actually have been brought against and paid by the funds. However, in other jurisdictions, at least two funds have failed due to inability to cover the claims brought against them.

b. The statutes governing the existing systems do not provide indemnification for legal and related expenses required to defend against a claim brought against registered property. Further, if a property loss is sustained, the legislation implies that the owner must go to court to establish the right to collect from the fund, incurring still further legal and related expenses. In addition, the maximum recovery available from the fund may be limited to a historic assessed value of the property that may be substantially below the market value at the time of the claim.

13. The process of obtaining initial registration of land is expensive and time-consuming:

a.   The act of registration requires a judicial proceeding. In the jurisdictions studied, the estimated minimum cost for a normal,uncontested registration application ranged across the jurisdictions from $555 to $1,500,[a] and the time for processing from six to eighteen months.

b.   Where registration applications are contested, both the time and cost involved can increase substantially.

14.   Torrens systems require high-quality administration for successful operation. As a result, the systems are expensive to operate and have required public subsidies to cover operating losses:

a.   Inadequate administration has contributed to the failure of many past Torrens systems. Unlike the conventional real-property systems, in which the deed-records office serves primarily as a repository of information, the public office in a Torrens system exercises quasi-judicial functions and requires appropriate professional and managerial competencies.

b.   As a result, current public fees for the filing and processing of transfers and interests affecting registered land range from 75 percent to 200 percent higher than comparable recording fees.

c.   Even these higher fees do not cover the operating costs of the systems. In the jurisdictions studied, to prevent deficits, revenue from Torrens fees must be supplemented either by surplus funds from the conventional recording function or from general tax revenues. Without these subsidies, fees would range from 200 percent to 300 percent higher than recording fees, and initial registration costs also would increase markedly.

15.   Limitations inherent in a bureaucratic system often slow down or otherwise impede the completion of real estate transactions:

a.   Torrens systems have been slow to adapt to such innovations as condominiums and to such new problems as those presented by air rights.

b.   Some systems have major backlogs of work. One system, for example, was twenty-three weeks behind in preparing certificates as of August 1977.

c.   The need to adhere to legislatively prescribed administrative procedures limits the ability of Torrens systems to respond to situations promptly and flexibly.

16.   As a general rule, Torrens produces no significant reduction in title-related residential closing costs. For the most part, the closing costs for home-owner Torrens property are similar to those for comparable unregistered

---

[a]As this book was in its final editing stages, we learned that a bill had been introduced in the Illinois legislature to increase the public registration fee from $30 to $1,000 in order for the Cook County Torrens System to recover current operating expenses (House Bill 3021, Illinois House of Representatives, 1978 Session, April 18, 1978). Presumably, this would include the current $115 estimated average charge for abstracting (see table 6-3 and the accompanying text in chapter 6) and would have the effect of almost tripling the minimum cost for initial registration in Cook County, from $574 to $1,429 (still below the current costs in Massachusetts).

property. In some cases, the title-related closing costs for homeowner Torrens property are slightly smaller; in others, they are somewhat greater.

This is so because Torrens does not obviate the need for professional assistance for search and examination of title and for title insurance where it would be otherwise required (see findings 9 and 10) and because registration filing costs are universally greater than comparable deed-recording fees (see finding 14).

There is a potential saving in the professional time required for search and examination of a registered title, but this saving rarely exceeds an hour and is only infrequently translated into a reduction in title-related expenses for closing of residential property.

Elimination of the subsidies that support the existing Torrens systems would only increase the extra cost for the Torrens filings and lead to a reduction (probably elimination) of the small saving in search and examination costs that now is only infrequently realized.

Conclusions

1. The total experience of American jurisdictions with the Torrens approach to establishing and transferring land ownership is essentially negative. The overall picture is one of failure to attract the interest of landowners, failure to recognize and carry out the administrative and financial obligations inherent in operating a complex system affecting important legal interests, and failure to fulfill original expectations.

In the few American jurisdictions that have had a continued experience over time with land registration, the Torrens approach has not emerged as a general-purpose mechanism for establishing and transferring interests in land. Its viability depends on its legal ability to perform special corrective functions with regard to title and boundary defects. These functions enable existing Torrens systems to continue to complement, in a limited fashion, the conventional real-property system. The experience is that Torrens is not a substitute for the conventional system; nor is Torrens claimed to be by those who currently know and use it when deemed appropriate.

The broader role of Torrens that was envisioned by its late-nineteenth-century proponents has been filled by other title-assurance mechanisms in combination with conventional recording systems. Torrens has been unable to compete with this approach because, for most purposes, it offers fewer benefits at equal or greater cost.

2. Torrens played a valuable role in some areas early in this century. However, the primary need that it fulfilled—facilitation of initial development of land under the pressures of rapid urban growth—has lost much of its significance. The surviving systems continue to be used for purposes related to

title defects. But if these systems did not already exist, it is unlikely that they would be created for those purposes today.

The Torrens systems in Massachusetts, Minnesota, and Cook County, Illinois, have been used primarily to free land from clouds on title history and, in the case of Massachusetts, to clarify boundaries. These were not necessarily the functions envisioned by those who imported the concept from other English-speaking jurisdictions, but they were the functions that attracted landowners and others interested in urban development. In each case, Torrens was instituted in response to uniquely local circumstances creating land-title needs that were less acutely felt in other urban areas.

Since the turn of the century, three generations of development have materially reduced the amount of land subject to uncertainty of title or lacking adequately recorded title histories. This is evidenced by a pattern of continuing decline in new land registrations (a practical cessation in Cook County) and the shift in Torrens system resources toward the administration of routine and special circumstances concerning land registered in earlier periods.

Where title problems suited to Torrens do occur in these jurisdictions, new registrations continue to be sought, albeit on a much smaller scale than in the past. In jurisdictions where Torrens does not exist, the same problems are dealt with by other means: improvements in judicial mechanisms for quieting title; advances in the technologies relied upon for surveying; and statutory solutions to specific kinds of title problems or the more general marketable title acts, which minimize or eliminate certain risks arising from events in earlier periods.

One current use of Torrens deserves special mention. For a large-scale commercial or industrial project involving the assembly of multiple land parcels, the cost of land registration is more than offset by the gains in simplification of complex legal title documents and in elimination of unusual title problems or of a minute gap in the boundary-line assembly process. The legal convenience and availability of a subsidized Torrens system can make it attractive to a large-scale developer. This use takes advantage of the fact that Torrens exists, but it would probably not be considered a sound economic or social basis to justify the creation of Torrens anew. Considering the public subsidies required to meet the operating costs of the current systems, such use raises serious questions of social policy.

3. Torrens' lack of success in the United States is best explained by its failure to eliminate the need for search and abstracting of title history, for professional examination of the title and related circumstances that may affect it, and, where required, for the risk-coverage features of title insurance. Nor does the Torrens approach prevent title defects from arising between transfers of ownership or eliminate the need for clearance measures to correct such defects once they occur. These limitations are inherent in the Torrens approach and are not the result of compromise or of inadequacies in legislative language.

The search and examination functions continue to be necessary for transfers of registered property, because the Torrens certificate does not identify all potential claims against the property that properly are of concern to a buyer or lender, nor does it in all cases override other interests. Further, the information reported on the Torrens certificate is not sufficient to inform even a trained attorney of the full nature and implications of nonownership interests that might exist. For residential property generally, search and examination functions are somewhat easier to perform if the title is registered, but the best that Torrens can accomplish is a small reduction in the amount of time required—a reduction that is only infrequently translated to a saving in expense. In fact, a typical transaction involving already registered residential property is, on the average, likely to have closing costs that are about the same or higher than those of comparable unregistered property.

While publicly maintained assurance or indemnification funds are a central part of the Torrens approach, the risk coverage provided by these funds is limited compared with the protections available from private insurance. This is because of Torrens' exclusive applicability to title issues, its failure to protect against risks arising from certain competing interests in land, and the limited kinds of injuries and losses it covers. In contrast, title insurance can offer protections against additional risks inherent in a transfer of land, whether title-related or otherwise (and whether ascertainable or not), and can include coverage for additional possible injuries and losses. For the lender or investor in a residential mortgage, title insurance offers the critical assurance of the mortgage's validity and enforceability and of its relative priority over other interests in the same property, items wholly beyond the scope of the Torrens certificate.

Finally, the title insurance mechanism frequently includes a variety of services designed to facilitate the timely and effective completion of real-estate transactions. In some areas, it is relied upon for search and examination and other basic services—at times, to the exclusion of the services of private attorneys—as well as for its risk-coverage features. Thus, Torrens and private insurance differ in services offered as well as in the quality and quantity of risk protection and loss indemnification. For all of these reasons, a residential transaction involving registered property is about as likely to be covered by title insurance, consistent with local practices and customs, as is its unregistered equivalent.

4.   The registration of a typical parcel of residential real estate is an unwise investment from the viewpoint of the homeowner. The cost of obtaining registration is high, and the benefits that accrue from registration status are substantially circumscribed. Without compelling circumstances that negatively affect the marketability of real property, there is little to identify in registration as a tangible benefit to the homeowner.

Since conventional mechanisms for title assurance are necessary whether or not property is registered, Torrens neither delivers nor can reasonably be expected to deliver any substantial benefit to the homeowner in the way of a cost saving in closing a transfer. In cases where a reduction in the efforts required for search and examination does result in a small cost reduction, the saving, even if passed on, is usually eroded by Torrens' higher administrative filing and processing fees. When no saving in search and examination is realized, the increased public charges for Torrens result in closing costs that are higher for registered residential property than for comparable unregistered property.

Thus, typical residential closing costs for transfers of registered property are about the same as or higher than those for unregistered property. This is true even though the present Torrens systems are operating at a deficit. The fee increases necessary to eliminate the deficits would ensure that the average Torrens residential transfer will rarely have lower closing costs than its unregistered equivalent.

Finally, if the substantial initial registration cost is taken into account, there can be no saving at all. Even with the current subsidy, the maximum possible reduction in closing costs for the first transfer after registration is only a small portion of the expense a homeowner must bear to obtain registration. Further, the present value of the maximum possible reduction of all future closing costs can never equal the investment in the form of initial registration costs. Accordingly, Torrens is an unwise investment from the viewpoint of society as a whole as well as from the parochial view of the individual homeowner.

5.   The foregoing considerations lead us to conclude that Torrens is not a sound concept for implementation in the United States today. The justification for the existing programs seems to lie in their abilities to continue to meet the occasional demands of commercial and industrial users, not those of the average homeowner and certainly not the broader societal demand for achieving reductions in residential closing costs. The subsidy to large developers from the general taxpayer—including the homeowner—is inherently regressive.

Existing inefficiencies in conventional real-property mechanisms do not support an argument for the implementation of Torrens. Fundamental improvements can be made without the certain expense, cumbersome administrative apparatus, and highly circumscribed benefits of Torrens. Current experiments with the automation of land record-keeping functions may provide evidence of additional improvements that can be made.

Any jurisdiction contemplating the introduction of a Torrens system should test carefully its hypotheses and promises against the substantial history of actual experience available in this nation. Those who have proposed the establishment of a mandatory Torrens system, to the exclusion of landowner option, have the heavy responsibility of justifying that position in the face of the administrative, economic, and practical issues analyzed in this book, as well as dealing with the socioeconomic issues of the value of free choice and the availability of competing alternatives.

1 Introduction

Background

This book provides a review and analysis of the experience in the United States with Torrens land-registration systems. Named after the premier of South Australia who instituted such a system in 1858, Torrens first came to this country toward the end of the nineteenth century. It appeared as a reform alternative to the mixture of substantive real-property law and public recording systems that continues to this day to be the predominant approach to governmental control over ownership and other legal interest in real property.

The basic features of the Torrens concept are described in detail in chapter 2. For introductory purposes, Torrens is best described as an approach to the establishment and transfer of land ownership whereby the government certifies the ownership interest. In so doing, the government also regulates the format through which certain other interests in the property must be expressed if they are to have any legal validity. The device involved is an official certificate, maintained by a public official usually called the Registrar. The certificate attests to the ownership and lists or briefly describes some of the other interests that exist or are claimed to exist. In contrast, the governmental role under the conventional system is limited to providing depositories for documentation of ownership and other claims and interests in real properpty. Relying in part on the information in these depositories, parties to a land transaction assume the responsibility for the determination of their own legal rights and responsibilities.

If the volume of legislation and literature generated is an accurate index, Torrens received considerable attention in the United States in the years between 1895 and 1915. Altogether, twenty-one states enacted legislation or constitutional amendments authorizing the Torrens approach. However, by the time of the depression, it was apparent that most of the programs that were actually started (perhaps more than 200) either had failed or had not been used to any significant extent. The overall collapse of the real estate market during the depression generated a temporary renewal of interest in the Torrens approach. Several studies were done and articles were written, but no new legislation resulted and nothing was done to revitalize dormant programs. In fact, some of the earlier statutory authorizations had already been repealed.

After the depression, again if the volume of literature affords any measure of the vitality of ideas, the interest in Torrens appears to have died for approximately another thirty years. Toward the late 1960s, it experienced yet another, but weaker, revival. In the intervening years, however, there was a substantial change in the motivations underlying the interest in Torrens.

The earlier literature suggests that Torrens initially attracted the attention of an intellectual reform movement concerned with perceived inadequacies in substantive real-property law. Political momentum was generated by practical considerations arising from the time and expense involved in establishing and/or clearing titles for land development during the intensive urbanization taking place at the turn of the century. Pressures for rapid expansion at that time required the commercial development of land that previously had been considered of little value and frequently had an inadequate record basis for validating ownership status.

In contrast, the current literature demonstrates an almost exclusive focus on the closing costs associated with transfers of homeowner property. The current Torrens proponents find support for their position in a body of literature that stresses inadequacies in the recording systems commonly relied on for public notice of the existence of ownership and other claims and interests in land. The proposition appears to be that Torrens, or something like it, can correct the recording deficiencies and, in turn, produce a substantial reduction in the title-related aspects of residential closing costs. Against this is a finding of a 1972 American University study:

There are a limited number of U.S. jurisdictions which have adopted a somewhat similar [Torrens] system, but their systems still require extensive title checking and only a few of that number use it to any noticeable degree.[a]

It is in response to this difference of opinion on the impact of Torrens that this study was undertaken. Accordingly, the study was conducted primarily from the viewpoint of the residential landowner. Our investigation focused on real-world experiences; our objectives were to learn how Torrens works in practice, what purposes of landowners it serves, and what impact it has on the land itself, on immediate landowners, and on others, including subsequent purchasers. Since Torrens systems in the United States have always been offered on a voluntary basis, we sought to identify the reasons why landowners elect to use Torrens, the kinds of land and owners most likely to be involved, and any changes in landowner interests or needs that might have occurred over the years. And, since residential closing costs were a critical

---

[a]Burke, B., and N. Kittrie, *The Real Estate Settlement Process and Its Costs,* A Report to the Department of Housing and Urban Development and the Veterans Administration, Reprinted in Hearings before the Subcommittee on Housing of the Committee on Banking and Currency, House of Representatives, Ninety-Second Congress, Second Session, on H.R. 13,337, Part 2, 843 (1972).

issue, we studied the economic impacts on typical homeowner property. Thus, the questions we sought to answer constituted a generalized cost/benefit analysis of Torrens.

Study Methodology

Our approach to this inquiry was largely empirical. An initial review of the literature identified three major urban areas in the continental United States that have had continuing experience with Torrens—Boston, Chicago, and the twin cities of Minneapolis and St. Paul. We reviewed the statutes, case law, and literature applicable to each and, in turn, visited each of the areas. Interviews were conducted with appropriate personnel responsible for the respective programs; judges and practicing lawyers; officers of major primary mortgage-lending institutions and of title companies; authors of current literature; and others whose local experience seemed appropriate. Since we viewed the legal profession as the group with the most representative source of information on user motivation, perceived benefits, closing costs, and so forth, our interview program included a representative mix of appropriate client constituencies, that is, lawyers who respectively represented investors, mortgage lenders, developers, and consumer buyers and sellers.

The principal investigators and authors of this study were a lawyer and an economist. This combination of disciplines and perspectives has not previously been brought to the subject. Others who contributed to our effort provided additional insights from still other backgrounds and experiences. The fact that one of the systems studied was in our home area proved useful. One of the principal investigators owns and lives on registered property, as do colleagues, friends, and neighbors. This permitted insights into consumer perspectives that would have been difficult to achieve otherwise. Our proximity to one of the major existing Torrens systems also enabled a broader exploration of the subject with lawyers and other real-estate specialists directly affected by land registration.

After the completion of our interviews, the reports now included as chapters 4, 5, and 6 of this book were drafted. Each of these deals in detail with one of the three areas studied. The drafts were then made available to the chief legal officers of each Torrens program for review and comment. Where appropriate, our initial drafts were modified to incorporate their observations. Since the information in these chapters comprises our core data base, our interest was in assuring both accuracy and comprehensiveness.

With the benefit of this knowledge, we then assessed the literature available on the other American jurisdictions that have attempted to utilize Torrens. We also reviewed literature available on the experience of Great Britain with a similar but mandatory system. Initially, we had decided not to examine foreign jurisdictions because of the difficulty of making valid comparisons in situations involving distinctly different legal systems, cultural attitudes, and historical patterns with respect to land use and ownership. However, we found that Britain's 75-year history with compulsory land registration was sufficiently relevant to be worthy of some attention.

Finally, we examined developments in the computerization of land record-keeping functions. Modern information-processing technologies offer substantial promise for accurate and efficient storage and retrieval of land-related data. However, there is some confusion in the current literature between the automation of land-registration systems and the use of data-processing techniques for ownership records and for other land-related information purposes. At present, the actual experience with the computerization of comprehensive land-records systems is limited.

Organization of the Book

To do justice to the complexity of the subject matter and to allow for differing readership interests, this work is organized into three distinct, and possibly separable, units:

The summary is separate and apart from the body of the book and consists of a brief statement of our findings and conclusions and the study's purpose and scope.

Chapters 2 and 3 are, respectively, observational and evaluative; that is, chapter 2 describes how Torrens systems have evolved and currently operate in the United States, and chapter 3 examines their uses, limitations, and economic impacts. The materials in these two chapters are drawn primarily from the factual detail in the later chapters and secondarily from the literature. They are the foundation for the summarized findings and conclusions.

Chapters 4 through 7 provide the detailed factual basis for the study. The first three describe the historical, operational, and resulting practical experiences of the U.S. jurisdictions studied intensively. Chapter 7 describes the experience with Torrens in other American jurisdictions, the British experience, and current developments in the computerization of land records.

We recommend that the thorough reader—one anxious to understand in depth the variations distinguishing the experience with Torrens in different states—begin his or her reading with chapters 4 through 7. After the details have been digested, chapters 2 and 3 will then provide a comprehensive review and evaluation of the Torrens experience.

Other readers may find the detail—particularly that in chapters 4, 5, and 6—unexciting and somewhat repetitious. For this group, we recommend at a minimum that chapters 2 and 3 be thoroughly studied. Chapter 2 presents a synthesis of the information in chapters 4 through 6 by describing a "typical"

Torrens system based on the characteristics of the major systems studied. The synthesis was created to illustrate the workings of a Torrens operation and to distill the different experiences into a single digestible format. The summary, of course, will be valuable to any reader to refresh recollections of information contained in the other chapters and to capsulize key findings and conclusions. An annotated bibliography is presented at the end of the book.

Terminology

Torrens is essentially a complex legal system. Most of the worthwhile literature on the subject is in legal periodicals. The statutes involved tend to run to more than 100 detailed sections. Furthermore, since Torrens amounts to a super-imposition on the particularly intricate body of real-property law, the statutes rely heavily on terminology that may be confusing or incomprehensible to non-legal readers who are interested in the broader subject.

Throughout this book, we have attempted to avoid the use of narrow legal terminology. This is consistent with the overall thrust of our inquiry, which was to view Torrens in a practical light, as it affected people as property owners, sellers and buyers, lenders, investors, builders, and so forth. Torrens laws are a bundle of legalisms, but Torrens has significance only as it affects the lay user. Thus, we attempted to confine the terminology used here to expressions con-noting understandable concepts: ownership interests, rather than fee simple variations; and other (lesser) interests, rather than the infinite variety of tech-nical legal rights that are intended to be generally included therein. Throughout we use the expression *claims and interests* to describe these lesser nonowner-ship interests. *Claims* are simply what the word implies—assertions that still must be proved and perfected to be legally valid. *Interests* are presumed valid, in that they comply with legal prerequisites and are manifested in formal docu-ments. Certain terms—such as mortgage, lien, judgment, easement, and encum-brance—were sometimes unavoidable. However, our intent was to confine their use to a minimum and to contexts that were not likely to be confusing.

We refer the lawyer, who understandably might wish information of a more legalistic nature, to the bibliography. There is no lack of legal articles on the Torrens question. Indeed, this study was motivated in part by the fact that much of the existing literature is confined to the purely legal aspects with comparatively little available on practical considerations.

Finally, we have used the words *Torrens* and *registration* or *registered land* to express an identical concept. This is intentional. *Torrens* is hardly a household word and *Torrenized* or *Torrenization,* while descriptive, are foreign to the language. Thus, we elected to resort to the more generic word form of *registration* without abandoning entirely the Torrens reference.

2

History and Current Operations

Origins and History

The Torrens approach to the establishment and transfer of ownership interests in real property—utilizing an official certificate to certify ownership and to provide notice of certain other claims and interests in the property—is named after Sir Robert Torrens. An Adelaide customs official who became the first premier (1857) and then registrar-general (1858) for the Territory of South Australia, Sir Robert is believed to have modeled his approach to land titles on the method used by the British Ships Registry for recording ownership interests in ships. Although there is evidence that variations in land registration were already in use in several European nations, the 1858 South Australian legislation was sufficiently attractive to serve as a model for many other British colonies and to perpetuate the use of the Torrens name as an acceptable English-language descriptor of the process.

The experiments of Torrens in South Australia coincided with a period of social unrest in Great Britain and much dissatisfaction with the prevailing legal system. With few local exceptions, England had not developed recording systems of the kind for real-property interests that had emerged in the American colonies as early as the seventeenth century. Real-estate ownership and transfer were considered purely private matters, a fact that lent support to the view that the law was perpetuating the wealth and political power of a feudal aristocracy. This system of "private conveyancing" was one of many attributes of the English legal system attacked by Charles Dickens in his famous 1853 novel, *Bleak House.*

It seems likely, then, that Robert Torrens was motivated by a desire to avoid repeating the problems being experienced in the mother country. The rapid succession of adoption of the Torrens approach by other British territories—for example, British Honduras in 1859; Vancouver Island, later British Columbia, in 1860; Tasmania in 1862; New South Wales in 1862; Ireland in 1865; New Zealand in 1870—indicates a predilection or willingness to experiment that could hardly have been based on an evaluation of accumulated experience since the first 1858 legislation in South Australia. In any event, the approach had spread to many English-speaking jurisdictions, including the western provinces of Canada, before it reached the United States.

Great Britain herself engaged in a series of unsuccessful attempts at land registration between 1862 and 1925. A modified compulsory system implemented in the London area in 1902 achieved little more than the registration of documents evidencing possession of land, a system not unlike that used to record documents in the American states. In 1925 the current British compulsory land registration system was initiated in conjunction with sweeping reforms in real-property law. However, fulfillment of the goal of universal registration is still many years away.

In the United States, use of the Torrens approach was authorized by constitutional amendment or legislative enactment in twenty-one states. Since the basic scheme pursued allowed autonomous county units, there was probably authorization for close to 1,000 different Torrens systems. Although no reliable data are available, we suspect that actual implementation was attempted by less than 25 percent of the eligible counties. Due to nonexistent or low-use patterns resulting from a combination of several factors—lack of need, poor administration, or the availability of preferable alternatives—the overwhelming majority of the attempted systems failed. The enabling legislation was repealed in some states. In others, programs simply obsolesced and the land involved was allowed to be withdrawn from the registration system.

Altogether twenty states enacted Torrens legislation. Six—California, Mississippi, Oregon, South Carolina, Tennessee, and Utah—subsequently repealed the enabling legislation. Notable among these are California, which repealed its legislation in 1955 based on a history of maladministration and little significant use, and Oregon, which repealed its authorization in 1972 because of the lack of current use and complaints of confusion by county officials. The other four states repealed their legislation much earlier, apparently because of lack of use. Still another state, Pennsylvania, failed to enact enabling legislation after an authorizing constitutional amendment.

In the remaining fourteen states, it is reported that four—Nebraska, North Dakota, South Dakota, and Virginia—made little or no use of the legislation. In another five where enabling legislation still exists—Colorado, Georgia, New York, North Carolina, and Washington—only infrequent use was made of the Torrens systems established in specific parts of the respective states. It appears that there has been hardly any use in recent times.

Hawaii, Illinois, Massachusetts, Minnesota, and Ohio are the only states in which Torrens has had any significant experience over time. In these five states, only a handful of Torrens systems continue to operate today with any degree of viability. Two of them operate statewide, under the auspices of the land courts of Hawaii and Massachusetts, respectively—the former having initially been created on the basis of the latter. The others are county systems operated in Cook County (Chicago)—the only system authorized in Illinois—and in many parts of Minnesota. The principal Minnesota systems are in Hennepin (Minneapolis) and Ramsey (St. Paul) counties. It is reported that two or three systems continue to operate in Ohio, but their existence is largely predicated upon the administration of land registered in prior decades.

Most American Torrens legislation was enacted between 1895 and 1915.

A survey of the legal literature published around the turn of the century reveals that the Torrens concept appeared attractive primarily because of a generalized interest in the simplification of real-property law and specific concerns about the capacity of existing recording systems to handle efficiently the increasing volumes of transactions arising from rapid urban growth. References to legislative conflicts suggest that the populism of that period provided some momentum for enactment. Although farming groups were active supporters of Torrens in many states, there was little actual use of its features in rural areas.

In some states, Torrens was appealing because of problems with land-title histories arising from circumstances unique to local areas. In Illinois, the major reason was the loss of public records occasioned by the 1871 Chicago fire. In Hawaii, the interest was in clarifying native titles based on legal precepts and customs that differed from American law. Southern California landowners had similar problems with Spanish land-grant histories.

Whatever the original rationales in the individual states, the subsequent history of Torrens shows that it was used with some degree of frequency primarily in urban areas—Boston, Buffalo, Chicago, Cincinnati, Cleveland, Los Angeles, and the Twin Cities. The states that subsequently repealed their enactments or made, at best, only infrequent use of Torrens were those that were predominantly rural in character. Even in those states with urban implementation of Torrens, its usage did not extend to all urban areas. New York City and San Francisco are examples of major cities that never pursued Torrens despite the existence of state authorization. San Francisco lost its public records to fires accompanying the 1906 earthquake but, unlike Chicago, did not turn to Torrens. Instead, title problems occasioned by the loss were dealt with through relief afforded by a special burnt records (McEnerney) act.

In many urban areas where Torrens was used to any extent, most of the land involved was registered prior to 1930. The collapse of real-estate markets during the depression stimulated a renewal of interest in Torrens, but this interest neither spawned new legislation nor vitalized existing programs. Studies performed during this period revealed a pattern of low public acceptance and discouraging administrative performance. The most notable of these studies— a comprehensive analysis by Professor Powell of the Columbia University Law School, *Registration of the Title to Land in the State of New York* (1938)[a]— concluded that there were no reforms that could improve the poor showing of Torrens in New York, short of a massive revision of substantive real-property law. Powell recommended that the Torrens legislation be repealed. The legislation was not repealed, but the limited experimentation with Torrens in New York ended.

---

[a]Despite its title, Powell's work covered the Torrens experience in all states. The study is cited many times throughout this book.

The overall experience shows that land-registration systems have not worked well in the United States even though comparable systems are widely accepted in some other English-speaking jurisdictions. Significant historical differences among the various jurisdictions experimenting with Torrens help to explain the wide divergence in acceptance. The early Torrens systems developed in Australia, and subsequently adopted in the western Canadian provinces and other parts of the late-nineteenth-century British Empire, were implemented at a time of sparse settlement. Much of the land was claimed by the Crown, and the registration program was fostered as part of governmental development and settlement programs. The lack of substantial preexisting private land-ownership patterns and histories presumably made it easy to establish new legal predicates for land ownership. It is noteworthy that the eastern Canadian Maritime Provinces, which had early settlement histories comparable to those of our New England states, are only now beginning to explore the use of land registration.

In England—which had never developed the recording systems of the American states—Torrens fared poorly as long as it was voluntary. After decades of legislative amendments, official studies, and little use, land registration was finally adopted as a mandatory national program, but only in conjunction with sweeping reforms abolishing many of the intricacies we associate with real-property law. Since the American states had already developed workable deed-recording systems by the time Torrens legislation was introduced, land registration had to compete on the basis of its capability to simplify problems in substantive real-property law. As it turned out, only a handful of areas with particular kinds of problems actually needed the relief to land-title problems that Torrens offered.

How Torrens Works

Torrens is frequently viewed as an alternative to the recording of various real-property interests. This is misleading, since it fails to appreciate Torrens' essential features. Torrens, or land registration, is an alternative method for establishing and transferring ownership interests in real property. Its technique for recording certain nonownership claims and interests differs from that of the traditional system, but the difference is of secondary importance only. Of greater importance are Torrens' distinctive approach to the concept of ownership and the singular role the government plays in implementing that concept.

Under the predominant American approach to real-property ownership, the government's role is limited to providing (1) legal standards that define and govern ownership and the relationships among parties that affect the property; (2) information systems containing records (and related indexes) of claims and interests that may legally attach to the property; and (3) judicial processes to ensure the maintenance of legal standards. A buyer takes title from his or her seller on the basis of a deed executed in conformance with legal standards, but must take steps independent of governmental processes to identify and evaluate the nature of the interest the seller is conveying. The deed is then recorded and indexed to signal the new ownership to others.

The Torrens system enlarges these traditional governmental functions by assuming additional responsibilities for establishing and transferring ownership interests. These responsibilities are fulfilled by a registration process whereby a governmental body (initially a court under American statutes) certifies ownership status. An official certificate issued by the government is the only acceptable device for proving ownership and for effecting a legal transfer of ownership. This certificate also reflects certain other claims and interests that attach to the property. Thus, the certificate is both the legal determinant of ownership status and the record of some, but not all, nonownership interests that may exist or be under claim.

It is a bit simplistic, but not inaccurate, to say that Torrens is property-oriented while the traditional American approach is owner-oriented. Torrens defines ownership in terms of the property involved and depends on the existence of a government certificate to translate the physical existence of the property into a legal right that has personal meaning. In contrast, the traditional approach defines ownership in terms of individual rights and entitlements and lets those rights, in turn, be transferred through negotiated exchanges that take place outside the sphere of government influence.

In both systems, the broad legal standards are the same, public records are kept, and individual interests are consensually exchanged through the vehicle of a legal document known as a deed. Under Torrens, however, the title certificate is all-powerful, and the buyer with a deed from a seller is not the true legal owner until the requisites of the registration process have been fulfilled. In addition, the person designated as owner by the certificate is entitled to legal ownership status even though the facts may be to the contrary.

The owner orientation of the traditional system is sometimes considered to be epitomized by the grantor-grantee (seller-buyer) index commonly maintained by deed-recording offices. The grantor-grantee index is referenced to the parties to a transfer and enables one to trace the chain of title back through successive sellers and buyers and to identify the record book (volume and page) containing copies of the respective deeds on file. The property-based equivalent of the grantor-grantee index, known as a tract index, is referenced to property descriptors. Unlike the grantor-grantee index, a tract index may identify information on file in the recording office that is in addition to ownership status, for example, the existence of a mortgage.

The distinction between the two indexes lies in their respective information bases and the quantity of information stored, not in any substantive difference in the way ownership is established and transferred or in the governmental responsibilities being discharged. Increasingly, deed-recording offices are maintaining both a tract index and a grantor-grantee index. And, while a Torrens certificate resembles a tract index-type disclosure for a particular land parcel (in that it provides references to multiple interests on file in the Torrens office), indexes are still required to identify and locate an individual certificate. Thus, a Torrens office may maintain grantor-grantee and/or tract indexes similar to those of a deed-recording office.

From the standpoint of mechanics, there are several differences in the operation of the land-registration systems among the jurisdictions we examined. For the most part, however, the differences are not significant. Each system adheres to the same basic principles of Torrens. We observed applications of similar approaches to frequently recurring problems in addition to parallels in statutory language, despite some differences in administrative structure and arrangement.

In each jurisdiction, the registration process begins with a court proceeding. Initial registration of real property results in a judicial declaration of ownership that has the legal effect of extinguishing all undeclared interests, whether or not persons holding those interests are identifiable or available to participate in the proceeding. A series of early appellate decisions held that the due-process clause of the Fourteenth Amendment to the U.S. Constitution, along with state equivalents, required judicial control of the proceeding and attendant procedural safeguards for the protection of property rights.[b] This requirement distinguishes American land-registration systems from the original Torrens model, established in Australia and followed in other parts of the British Commonwealth, where the initial registration is handled administratively.

After initiation of the registration petition, the title history to the land is searched and an abstract prepared and examined by a qualified person (usually an official known as the chief examiner of titles) who reports to the court. This report relates directly to the status of the title and helps to identify potential defendants who might have a claim or interest in the property. After proper notice of the proceeding (including personal service, publication and posting), a hearing is held. While most petitions are uncontested, intervention by interested parties anxious to protect their interests (for example, abutting landowners) is not infrequent. The final decree issued by the court amounts to a declaration of title in the owner(s) subject to such other interests, for example, a mortgage, found by the court to be current. In Massachusetts (and occasionally in Minnesota), the decree extends to include boundary lines determined by an extensive survey and coordinated with reference to permanently fixed monuments; that is, both title and boundaries are registered.

The declaration of ownership (title) established by the registration decree

---

[b]See, e.g., *People* v. *Chase* 165 Ill. 527 (1896); see also *Eliason* v. *Wilborn*, 281 U.S. 547 (1930).

is considered to be indefeasible; that is, it is legally conclusive as to undeclared interests based on a prior event or occurrence. However, the legal conclusiveness is subject to certain exceptions. While there are some differences in the exceptions provided among the different jurisdictions, each recognizes:

interests based on current local or municipal taxes or assessments;

claims or interests based on the federal law or constitution (for example, claims arising from bankruptcy proceedings and tax liens, and claims against the property raised by Indian tribes under federal law);

mechanic's liens for a certain limited period of time; and

rights of parties in possession of the property.

In addition, the conclusiveness of the ownership interest declared by the initial registration decree may be challenged by appeal within a period of time that is considerably longer than that normally prescribed for litigation generally. This lengthy period for appeal accommodates persons who properly should have been named as a party to the original court proceeding.

Following completion of the court action, the initial registration decree is transferred to the office administering registered titles. The responsible officer is typically referred to as the registrar of titles and is frequently the same person who holds the elected county position of recorder of deeds. In this administrative office, the registration decree is recorded and stored and its legal effect merged into a formal certificate of title, which from then on is the primary determinant of ownership status and the existence of any nonexcepted claims or interests in the property.

This official certificate remains on file with the registrar. At the time of its preparation, a duplicate certificate is prepared and delivered to the registered owner. Figure 2-1 reproduces a Massachusetts Owner's Duplicate Certificate and is illustrative of those used in other jurisdictions. A transfer of the property by the registered owner (that is, the owner indicated on the face of the official certificate) can be effectuated only by presentation of a valid deed from the registered owner and the surrender of the duplicate certificate. The actual legal transfer takes place by cancellation of the old certificate and preparation of a new one in the name of the new owner. At that time, a new duplicate certificate is prepared and delivered to the new owner. Similar requirements exist if a transfer is to be accomplished by other than voluntary means. For example, if the transfer is to be made pursuant to a court order (for example, a probate decree), the registrar must have a certified copy of that order before a new certificate can be prepared.

Nonownership interests in land are treated in like fashion. Interests voluntarily conferred by the registered owner (such as mortgages) and those involuntarily incurred (such as liens from unsatisfied judgments) must be filed with the

CERTIFICATE
OF
TITLE.

Book....818......   *Page*....92........

No............137642...............

DATE OF REGISTRATION

May 15, 1972

Irving H. Plotkin, et ux
                           Owner s

SOUTH REGISTRY DISTRICT
OF
MIDDLESEX COUNTY,
MASSACHUSETTS.

IMPORTANT
———•———
See Note on back.
———•———

LAND COURT CASE NO.   27302

IMPORTANT

★ LAND REGISTRATION OFFICE
SOUTH REGISTRY DISTRICT OF MIDDLESEX COUNTY
(EAST) CAMBRIDGE, MASSACHUSETTS.

NOTE

This certificate must accompany every voluntary instrument relating to this property which is presented for registration at ★ this office.

This certificate should be mailed or delivered to ★ this office upon request when an involuntary instrument affecting this property is registered, so that the same may be noted hereon.

If this certificate is lost, a petition for a new one should be filed at once in the Land Court at Boston.

When a certificate owner dies, a petition for a new certificate after death should be filed in the Land Court at Boston, if the property goes to heirs or devisees.

FORM 28XLC 1/71

Figure 2-1. Massachusetts Torrens Certificate

Extract from Chapter 185, Section 46, of the General Laws, as amended.

Every petitioner receiving a certificate of title in pursuance of a decree of registration, and every subsequent purchaser of registered land taking a certificate of title for value and in good faith, shall hold the same free from all encumbrances except those noted on the certificate, and any of the following encumbrances which may be existing:

First, Liens, claims or rights arising or existing under the laws or constitution of the United States or the statutes of this commonwealth which are not by law required to appear of record in the registry of deeds in order to be valid against subsequent purchasers or encumbrances of record.

Second, Taxes, within two years after they have been committed to the collector.

Third, Any highway, town way, or any private way laid out under section twenty-one of chapter eighty-two, if the certificate of title does not state that the boundary of such way has been determined.

Fourth, Any lease for a term not exceeding seven years.

Fifth, Any liability to assessment for betterments or other statutory liability, except for taxes payable to the commonwealth, which attaches to land in the commonwealth as a lien; but if there are easements or other rights appurtenant to a parcel of registered land which for any reason have failed to be registered, such easements or rights shall remain so appurtenant notwithstanding such failure, and shall be held to pass with the land until cut off or extinguished by the registration of the servient estate, or in any other manner.

Sixth, Liens in favor of the United States for unpaid taxes arising or existing under the Internal Revenue Code of 1954 as amended from time to time. As amended St. 1963, c. 242, § 2.

Owner's Duplicate Certificate.

TRANSFER CERTIFICATE OF TITLE REGISTERED IN BOOK 818 **PAGE** 92   **No.** 137642

From Transfer   Certificate No. 114115 , Originally Registered   April 10, 1964 , **in Registration**

Book 700   **Page** 165   for the South Registry District of Middlesex County.

This is to Certify that

Irving H. Plotkin and Janet Bufe Plotkin

of **Lexington** in the County of **Middlesex** and Commonwealth of Massachusetts, **married**

to **each other,** **are** the owners in fee simple , as tenants by the entirety,

of that certain parcel of land   situate in **Lexington**

in the County of Middlesex and said Commonwealth, bounded and described as follows:

> Westerly by Baskin Road, one hundred and twenty-five feet;
> Northeasterly by lot 65 as shown on plan hereinafter mentioned,
>   one hundred thirty-seven and 71/100 feet;
> Easterly by lots 30 and 31 on said plan, one hundred and
>   forty-four feet;and
> Southwesterly by lot 63 on said plan, one hundred fifty-five
>   and 54/100 feet;

Said parcel is shown as lot 64 on said plan, (Plan No. 27302G).

All of said boundaries are determined by the Court to be located upon the ground as shown on a subdivision plan, as approved by the Court, filed in the Land Registration Office, a copy of which is filed in the Registry of Deeds for the South Registry District of Middlesex County in Registration Book 641, Page 50, with Certificate 102200.

The above described land is subject to restrictions as set forth in two deeds, one given by Neil McIntosh to Josephine P. Duba, dated May 25, 1945, duly recorded in Book 6858, Page 592, and the other given by Leonard E. Bennink to Augustus E. Scott, dated July 13, 1887, duly recorded in Book 2136, Page 5.

Figure 2-1. *Continued*

The above described land is subject to a Grant of Easement from Ernest J. Corrigan to New England Telephone and Telegraph Company and Boston Edison Company, Document 326035.

The above described land is subject to a Grant of Easements from Ernest E. Outhet et al Trustees to Town of Lexington to construct sewers &c. in, through and under Baskin Road, Document 355045.

And it is further certified that said land is under the operation and provisions of Chapter 185 of the General Laws, and any amendments thereto, and that the title of said

Irving H. Plotkin and Janet Bufe Plotkin

to said land is registered under said Chapter, subject, however, to any of the encumbrances mentioned in Section forty-six of said Chapter, and any amendments thereto, which may be subsisting, and subject also as aforesaid.

WITNESS, WILLIAM I. RANDALL Esquire, Judge of the Land Court, at Cambridge, in said County of Middlesex,

the fifteenth day of May the year nineteen hundred and seventy-two

at 1 o'clock and 50 minutes in the after- noon.

Attest, with the Seal of said Court,

Acting Assistant Recorder

Address of owner s: 55 Baskin Road, Lexington, Mass.

Land Court Case No. 27302

FORM 26 LC 2M .7/71

MEMORANDA OF ENCUMBRANCES ON THE LAND

Document Number.	Kind.	Running in Favor of.	Terms.
391122	Taking	Town of Lexington	Taking of easement in Baskin Road. Pl. with Doc.
497365	Mortgage	Lexington Federal Savings and Loan Association	$50,000. Principal and Interest payable as stated in mortgage.

Figure 2-1. *Continued*

DESCRIBED IN THIS CERTIFICATE. No. 137642

DATE OF INSTRUMENT.	DATE OF REGISTRATION.					SIGNATURE OF ASSISTANT RECORDER.	DISCHARGE.	
	YEAR & MONTH	D.	H.	M.	A. M. or P. M			
1963	1963							
Apr. 15	Apr.	24	10	35	AM	*George Holehman* ACTING		
1972	1972							
May 15	May	15	1	50	PM	*George Holehman* . ACTING		

registrar in order to be legally effective. The registrar enters descriptions of these interests on the official certificate. As figure 2-1 demonstrates, these descriptions, known as memorials, only briefly depict the nature of the interests filed.

For purposes of comparison, figure 2-2 is a reconstruction of the memorial page (memoranda of encumbrances) of the title certificate that preexisted the certificate shown in figure 2-1. While the information memorialized on the certificate might alert an intelligent layman to the possible existence of some kind of problem with the title, it is not adequate to inform even an experienced attorney about the true nature, status, or full implications of the nonownership interests reported. For example, note the nondischarged entry "Notice of Bill in Equity" on the memorial page in figure 2-2. This would alert an attorney to the need to ascertain the status of judicial proceedings and to identify and examine supporting documents before a responsible opinion could be rendered on the status of the title. In addition, the attorney would have to search for (and examine the significance of) the "excepted" interests described earlier.

The appearance of memorials on the certificate preserves whatever legal effectiveness the memorialized claims and interests may have and provides notice of their existence to interested parties. The memorial attests to both the existence of the claim or interest and its relative priority by time of filing with the registrar. The claim or interest is "registered" in the same sense that it would be "recorded" following the conventional approach of deed-recording systems. However, the memorial does not amount to certification of the validity, enforceability, or priority of the claim and interest described. The nature, extent, and effectiveness of any claim or interest memorialized are functions of the documents filed with the registrar and their supporting legal principles. For this reason the registrar, unlike a recorder of deeds, retains and stores the originals of all documents filed so that they are available for inspection and examination by those interested in the property. Persons claiming ownership or other legal interests in land must be content to retain copies of the documents supporting their claims.

The official certificate provides the legal infrastructure for the Torrens, or land-registration, system. The initial decree extinguishes all undeclared (and nonexcepted) claims or interests in the property as of the time of registration. The official certificate prepared pursuant to the decree, and those subsequently prepared to reflect each transfer of ownership, perpetuates the validity of the decree. The certificate also recites the existence of any subordinate claim or interest that may have been registered. A claim or interest not reflected on the certificate can have no legal effect against the property unless it is of a kind excepted by statute or judicial decision. As a matter of law, then, the certificate is the exclusive determinant of the ownership interest and of the threshold for enforceability of certain other claims and interests that can attach to the land.

A good-faith purchaser is entitled to rely on the information stated in and on the certificate as accurate and complete as to all nonexcepted interests.

Under the Torrens approach, an interest in land cannot be established by either adverse possession or prescription—legal mechanisms by which continued use over a period of time establishes a claim or entitlement to the land—since the use period involved is not susceptible to being filed and memorialized on the certificate. This preeminent position of the certificate and its entries also dictates that a clerical or administrative error or omission in the preparation of the certificate or a memorial can undercut the validity of an otherwise lawful interest. For example, a mortgage that is properly filed with the registrar, but not memorialized on the appropriate certificate, has no validity against a subsequent purchaser who had no knowledge of the existence of the mortgage.

The ownership interest in real property can also be lost because of an error or fraudulent inducement in the preparation of the official certificate. The Torrens statutes we examined all provide that a good-faith purchaser for value is entitled to rely on the declaration of ownership embodied in the official certificate to the exclusion of the interests of any "true" owner. The requirement for an owner's duplicate certificate exists not only to provide a vehicle for the transfer of ownership, but also to reduce the potential for error and fraud that is inherent in the administration and control of the all-powerful official certificate.

Without the requirement for the duplicate certificate, a certificate could be prepared in the name of a nonentitled owner who, in turn, could convey good title to an innocent purchaser who is legally entitled to rely on the certificate's declaration of ownership. Of course, the requirement for the duplicate certificate is hardly fail-safe. An unscrupulous person in the possession of a proper duplicate can forge a deed and register a fraudulent transfer; or both the duplicate and the deed can be forged.

This dominant role of the certificate, which is so central to the Torrens approach, places the registrar of titles and the landowner in a particular kind of dilemma. On the one hand, the statutes involved clearly deny the registrar the exercise of complete discretion in dealing with day-to-day situations. This is intended to discourage the potential for fraud or neglect with respect to the maintenance of the integrity of pieces of paper that are so thoroughly dispositive of important legal rights. On the other hand, the very nature of the Torrens concept demands that the registrar exercise quasi-judicial responsibilities with respect to the interpretation of legal documents, court orders, and the like, and in the application of judgment to deal with potential problems arising from clerical and typographical errors. The kind of administrative discretion that would allow opportunities to cure such predictable mistakes leaves room for fraud and neglect of established property rights.

Since the system is paper-intensive, it demands a high degree of quality in

MEMORANDA OF ENCUMBRANCES ON THE LAND

DOCUMENT NUMBER	KIND	RUNNING IN FAVOR OF	TERMS
391122	Taking	Town of Lexington	Taking of easement in Baskin Road. Pl. with Doc.
404031	Mortgage	Lexington Federal Savings and Loan Association	$60.000. Principal and Interest payable as stated in mortgage, covering this and other registered land.
418834	Mortgage	Lexington Federal Savings and Loan Association	$27,750. Principal and Interest payable as stated in mortgage.
457158	Mortgage	General Oil Company, Inc.	$25,000. Principal and Interest payable as stated in mortgage.
491577	Notice of Bill in Equity	Lexington Federal Savings and Loan Association	To exercise Power of Sale under Mortgage Document No. 418834.

Figure 2-2. Memorial Page of Certificate prior to Certificate in Figure 2-1

DESCRIBED IN THIS CERTIFICATE. No. 114115

DATE OF INSTRUMENT	DATE OF REGISTRATION					SIGNATURE OF ASSISTANT RECORDER	DISCHARGE
	YEAR & MONTH	D.	H.	M.	A.M. or P.M.		
1963 Apr. 15	1936 Apr.	24	10	35	AM	*Francis E. McKenner*	
1964 Apr. 10	1964 Apr.	10	3	0	PM	*Francis C. McKenner*	May 25, 1965. DISCHARGED BY DOCUMENT NO. 418833 *Benedict Brady* Asst. Recorder.
1965 May 24	1965 May	25	12	10	PM	*Benedict Brady*	
1968 July 17	1968 July	18	3	0	PM	*A. L. Buckley*	
1971 Nov. 3	1971 Nov.	4	11	10	AM		

the administration of the title certificate. But it also appears to demand a degree of inflexibility that inhibits effective dealing with new or infrequently recurring situations where there is little or no precedent to support predictable or probable outcomes. Thus, Torrens systems have experienced difficulties in dealing with such new applications to property interests as condominiums and interests in air rights.

With the exception of Massachusetts, where a special three-judge land court governs the administration of all changes to owner certificates, Torrens requires an allocation of responsibilities between the registrar's office and the courts for the handling of a variety of commonly encountered problems. Typically, an administrative officer designated the chief examiner of titles is entrusted to examine documents and hold hearings to authorize the replacement of lost duplicate certificates, the correction of errors, and the preparation of new certificates in a variety of situations—such as an owner's death, a divorce between joint owners, a change in an owner's name—where a change in circumstances causes the controlling certificate to reflect inaccurately the reality of ownership. If the facts are unclear or the law requires interpretation, the matter inevitably must be resolved by judicial processes.

In each jurisdiction, an assurance or indemnity fund is established by assessments of fees at the time of initial registration—usually one-tenth of one percent of the assessed value of the land involved—for the purposes of compensating persons for injuries sustained as a result of system operations. The original contemplation was that this fund would be used to compensate persons for property interests erroneously cut off at the time of the initial registration decree. This has occasioned the bankruptcy of more than one fund, but, in the jurisdictions we examined, this kind of claim has been almost nonexistent. Instead, the practical purpose of the various funds has been to compensate for injury caused by mishaps or errors in certificate administration. However, the size of the funds is surprisingly small considering the length of time in operation and the value of the land involved. Moreover, statutory limitations and uncertainties as to the recovery available from the funds has tended to undermine their indemnification significance for landowners and investors.

Torrens in Operation: A Synthesis

Review of the various Torrens experiences set forth in the latter chapters of this book leaves one with the awareness of the care needed to distill the lessons these experiences offer. On the one hand, over seventy-five years of experience in Cook County, Illinois, in Massachusetts, and in the Twin Cities of Minnesota show that, with careful administration, land registration can and does fulfill certain specific purposes. On the other hand, these purposes are few and are being fulfilled by judicial and other methods elsewhere. No Torrens system has evolved into one of general-purpose application and the number of systems that have failed is overwhelming. The concept has certainly been well tested throughout the country.

The systems we examined are hardly typical of the Torrens experiments in the United States. To the contrary, the overall experience suggests that they represent only the most robust of their species. The evidence shows that their relative heartiness is *sui generis*, directly dependent upon combinations of historical events, local patterns in land development, and incidents of land-ownership and investor needs that are unique to their respective areas.

Since peculiarly local circumstances appear to be the dispositive factor in every case, the picture presented by any one of the existing Torrens operations is far from emblematic. For this reason, in this section we have constructed a realistic picture of a Torrens operation independent of the circumstances peculiar to any particular geographic area. By isolating the various legal, financial, and operational components that recur in the existing systems, we were able to create an archetypical system embodying a Torrens norm—a synthesis of existing experiences without the distortions or peculiarities of any actual system.

Our goal in this regard is to illustrate the operations and implications of Torrens in simple terms. In some instances, a single choice among competing alternatives was selected to illustrate an important attribute of the land-registration approach. Our synthesized system differs substantially from existing Torrens programs in only one important respect: it is economically self-sustaining, receiving no subsidy from general tax or other resources. In all cases, using commentary set off by asterisks and in different type size, we have attempted to explain the synthesized operation in terms of the features of the existing urban Torrens systems.

The City/County of Franklin, State of Lincoln

For illustration, we have created an urban area known as Franklin. For the sake of simplicity, the name applies to the core city as well as the county, there being a single metropolitan area. Franklin's Torrens operation coexists at the county level with a conventional real-property deed-recording system.

Franklin's current population is one million, a figure that has remained stable since the late sixties. Growth in the form of suburban development continues in contiguous counties, but the pattern shows signs of levelling off. Within Franklin's county limits there is still some farm and other undeveloped land that is slowly giving way to development. We intend Franklin to be typical of American urban areas. Its relative mix of economic activity (industrial, commercial, educational, and governmental) and of residential living patterns (apartment, single- and multiple-family, and condominiums) mirrors that for American urban areas generally.

Franklin is located in the state of Lincoln. Early in this century, Lincoln enacted legislation authorizing its counties to establish a Torrens system. The legislature considered a statewide system like that of Massachusetts, but rejected it in favor of county option because of the apparent lack of need in rural areas. Since Franklin was (and continues to be) the largest urban area in the state, it was the first county to implement a Torrens system. Others followed suit until about a quarter of the counties offered land registration. Few of these programs continue to operate today. Because of low use in many counties, and an outright failure involving the bankruptcy of one county insurance fund, the Lincoln Torrens law was amended in 1939 to allow the withdrawal of land from registration in all counties where the incidence of registration was less than 10 percent of land parcels. Due to this percentage cutoff, Franklin is the only county in which the withdrawal right does not exist.

* * *

The general circumstances and history painted here are intended to reflect the pattern common to most states authorizing Torrens, that is, enactment early in the century, provision for county option, and predominant use in rapidly expanding urban areas. Low or nonexistent use in less urban counties has been the rule, a fact that has led to much confusion because of a lack of experience in administering intricacies.

The bankruptcy of Torrens insurance funds occurred in California and Nebraska. It is used here to simulate an event giving rise to a fairly typical legislative revision. One statutory modification common to many Torrens states provided for the withdrawal of land from the registration system. The original Torrens statutes typically denied the opportunity to remove land from registration. However, as experience accumulated, withdrawal provisions were created, frequently to allow landowners to escape the burden of cumbersome administration in areas where little use was being made of the system. In Minnesota, for example, withdrawal is allowed in counties without a major city. In contrast, the Illinois statute does not provide for withdrawal. In Massachusetts, withdrawal is allowed only under limited circumstances related to the use of the land for condominiums.

* * *

Currently, Franklin has approximately 240,000 land parcels. Twenty-five percent, or 60,000 of these parcels, are registered. Historically, much of this land was placed in registration in the form of large tracts in preparation for development. The peak periods for the initiation of registration proceedings coincide with those of rapid development and expansion in Franklin—in the late 1910s and early 1920s and again in the late 1950s and early 1960s. With the gradual decrease in the rate of development beginning around 1965, the incidence of new registrations has steadily declined to the current average of approximately 100 per year.

The overwhelming majority of Franklin's recent registration applications involve commercial and industrial property. The few involving residential property are being initiated by developers planning to establish new residential units. It is rare for a homeowner to seek registration of existing residential property. However, the number of residences on registered land is increasing as a result of both new development and conversion to condominiums on land registered by prior owners.

* * *

This pattern of initial registrations, both historical and current, is substantially similar to that in the jurisdictions that have had any significant experience with Torrens. Each experienced phenomenal growth in the latter part of the nineteenth century, a pattern that continued through the first quarter of the twentieth century. The city of Chicago, which has had the most experience with Torrens, grew from an 1850 population of approximately 30,000 to almost 1.7 million persons in 1900, and over 3.37 million in 1930. Minneapolis and St. Paul grew from 1880 populations of almost 47,000 and 40,000, respectively, to 203,000 and 163,000 in 1900, and 381,000 and 235,000 in 1920. The more compact, but earlier settled, city of Boston grew from 135,000 in 1850 to 561,000 in 1900 to 748,000 in 1920.

Pressures from growth of this magnitude provided the political impetus for experimenting with Torrens and stimulated the registration of much of the land registered in each of the four cities today. During the depression of the 1930s, new registrations came to a virtual halt because of the lack of development. Expansion after World War II contributed to a renewal of registration applications. The postwar registrations tend to reflect the emphasis on the development of residential housing from large suburban tracts rather than the spurt in population that occasioned the earlier registrations. As this growth in suburban expansion has subsided, so has the frequency of new registration applications.

* * *

There have been two major revisions of Lincoln's Torrens legislation since its initial enactment. The first occurred in 1939 following publication of Professor Powell's New York study and a review of Lincoln's own programs after the bankruptcy mentioned earlier. Its principal change involved the authorization for withdrawal mentioned earlier. The second took place in 1966 after a series of claims against Franklin's insurance fund revealed substantial maladministration resulting from the patronage practices of a political machine that had dominated local government since the depression years.

The resulting scandal led to pressures to repeal the Torrens legislation. The legislature decided against repeal, but added the requirement for a supervisory mechanism insulating professional and executive positions from political appointments. The mechanism is an independent screening board consisting of representatives of the judiciary, the legal profession, real-estate interests, and consumers. The Lincoln legislature also made other changes intended to streamline the administrative operation of the Franklin program, to place it economically on a self-sustaining basis, and to rebuild the insurance fund to a respectable level. The experience of the past ten years supports the conclusion that these reforms have fulfilled their intended objectives.

As a practical matter, none of the 1966 revisions made any change in the substantive underpinnings of the Torrens approach. A proposal that the initial registration procedure be removed from the courts entirely was rejected on the basis of findings that constitutionally mandated safeguards for the protection of property rights would be most properly observed by the judicial system. It was also felt that overall judicial scrutiny was essential to prevent abuses of the kind that led to the legislative revisions. The interests in land excluded from Torrens coverage—for example, current taxes and assessments, unfiled mechanics liens, short-term possessory interests, and interests based on federal taxes and laws— were also continued without modification, despite proposals for a narrowing of the exceptions.

The 1966 revisions did make certain changes in the law with respect to the treatment of air rights over land, the registration of easements, and the processing of certificates for units of large subdivisions and condominiums. For the most part, however, these changes were facilitative in nature and addressed administrative bottlenecks that had developed under the prior legislation.

* * *

We use the vehicle of a political scandal to stage a hypothetical legislative review of a number of problems that have plagued various Torrens operations over the years. The independent screening board is a device to promote the competent and devoted administrative leadership required for an effective Torrens operation. Maladministration leading to excessive claims and a lack of public confidence led to the repeal of Torrens in California. Similar experiences in New York, although on a substantially lesser scale, led Professor Powell to conclude that successful operation depended on the utilization of a cadre of dedicated civil servants, a practice not fostered by urban political systems.

Current experiences tend to corroborate Powell's general observations. The high degree of respect and confidence we found for the respective registration systems in the Twin Cities and in Massachusetts appears to be directly attributable to the efforts of successive generations of dedicated and talented professionals. However, we encountered substantial criticism from lawyers in the Twin Cities area concerning the caliber of administration in some of the less urban Torrens systems in Minnesota. Further, we noted a lack of public confidence in the Cook County administration, which has contributed in part to a near cessation of new registrations.

We have assumed that once confronted with the need to rebuild a depleted insurance fund, the Lincoln legislature would reexamine the entire economic basis of the optional Torrens approach and conclude that it should operate without the public subsidy that characterizes existing programs. The particular changes involved are discussed later in the context of the specifics involved. The changes indicated for the treatment of condominiums, air rights, and easements are mentioned here to emphasize the administrative difficulties that some of the existing systems have had in adapting to certain changes in land-use patterns.

We have not assumed the need in Lincoln for any substantive changes to the fundamentals of the Torrens approach—initial registration by judicial proceeding and subsequent administration through the device of the controlling certificate—

because there seems to be none appropriate. None of the existing statutes demonstrates any significant changes of this type. Nor does there appear to be any problem in statutory approach or draftsmanship. The particular hardships created by some aspects of the registration system seem to be unavoidable cost trade-offs if the system's basic purpose of curing title defects is to be fulfilled.

* * *

The Current Operation

Franklin's Torrens system involves three different government offices. The Office of the Registrar is the administrative office responsible for the maintenance of certificates and the processing of transfers and other activities affecting registered land. The Office of the Chief Examiner of Titles is a quasi-judicial agency that processes applications for registration on behalf of the county court. It also serves as legal advisor on land registration to the registrar and to the judges of the county court, and acts in a judicial capacity on certain matters affecting registered land. The third governmental office is the county court, which issues registration decrees and has general supervisory authority over the entire registration apparatus.

* * *

This organizational arrangement reflects the prevailing pattern established by the different Torrens statutes enacted by American states. Because an initial registration decree has the legal effect of negating possible interests in the property, a series of early court decisions required the use of judicial processes in order to secure constitutional safeguards for the protection of property interests. Since subsequent experience has shown that this is not an onerous requirement, we assume that the Lincoln legislature would not attempt to disturb this tradition or risk a constitutionally impermissible result by assigning the registration function to an administrative body.

In practice, the Office of the Chief Examiner of Titles has emerged as the bridge of expertise in registration matters between the judicial functions of the court and the day-to-day administrative responsibilities of the registrar's office. In Massachusetts, the chief examiner's function is merged into an integrated administration headed by the specialized land court; in Cook County, the chief examiner's office is located within that of the registrar. In both cases, the chief examiner's responsibilities are substantially similar. We elected to keep the Franklin offices separate—which is the Minnesota approach—for the sake of clarity in illustration.

* * *

The Registrar's Office. The Franklin Office of the Registrar is an operating division within a consolidated county Department of Finance and Records Systems. Other operating divisions within this department, such as the conventional deed-recording system and the tax-assessing office, have different land-related responsibilities. The department is headed by the county financial officer, who is an elected official. The registrar, the administrative head of the Torrens office, is appointed by the county executive subject to the approval of the independent screening board required by the 1966 legislative revisions.

The 1977 budget for the registrar's office requires $280,000 for direct costs, that is, personnel, supplies, and equipment. Physical overhead—space and utilities—is not included, as these items are absorbed in the county's general budget for governmental support. An additional $28,000 is charged to the Torrens operation for administrative overhead—its share of the expenses required for the Office of County Financial Officer—bringing the total current annual cost to operate the system to $308,000.

The total staff of the registrar's office consists of twenty-one people. This number has remained constant for five years, although the budget has increased over 15 percent because of cost-of-living wage increases. The upturn in real-estate activity in 1976, after a lull of more than two years, placed a burden on the staff that continues. In mid-1977, the office was fifteen weeks behind in the preparation of new certificates, despite the assistance of three additional staff trainees funded by a federal CETA grant.

One of the 1966 legislative changes required that fees for the registrar's services be "reasonably" calculated in order to meet current operating expenses. Accordingly, fees were increased in 1976 because of substantial deficits incurred in 1974 and 1975 through a combination of increasing costs and reduced real-estate activity. The current fee structure assesses a total of $90 in charges for a routine transfer of residential property that is already registered:

$30 for the preparation of a new certificate and an owner's duplicate;

$15 for entering the satisfaction of the seller's mortgage;

$20 for the registration of the new mortgage;

$15, which is paid to the Chief Examiner's Office; and

$10, which is paid to the insurance fund.

The standard charge for other instruments requiring either removal or entry of a memorial on a certificate is $15.

The registrar anticipates that a mix of real-estate activity involving approximately 2,600 residential transfers, 1,700 other transfers, and 6,000 other documents affecting registered land will generate revenues of $276,000 in 1977. An additional $67,500 and $43,000 will be collected and paid to the chief examiner and the insurance fund, respectively.

* * *

The projected volumes of real-estate activity and related figures on budgetary needs and staff requirements are based on the experiences of the systems we examined. Although we found some difference among the four counties in the ratio of annual activity to the estimated numbers of registered parcels, there was substantial similarity in the costs required to handle comparable levels of activity. Thus, by striking an average among the four, we assume that Franklin's 60,000 registered land parcels will produce the level of activity projected for calendar year 1977. In turn, this activity will require an administrative staff of twenty-one people, with ranges in salary and needs for supplies and equipment dictating a $280,000 budget for direct costs.

The requirement that fees be calculated to recover operating expenses is not a common Torrens feature in the United States. In fact, we found that, with the possible exception of Cook County, the existing systems operate at a substantial loss, subsidized either by the conventional recording system or general county revenues. The subsidy has a regressive character, since the actual users of land registration are persons pursuing commercial purposes. We assume, therefore, that the Lincoln legislature would have opted to eliminate the subsidy and place the fiscal burden for the services involved directly on the users.

The effect is to increase substantially the fees for the services required for typical transactions. The $90 required for a routine Franklin residential trans-action is more than triple the amount currently charged in Massachusetts and Minnesota. It is, however, somewhat comparable to the charges required in Cook County, where fees were increased in 1976 in an attempt to reduce the subsidy and to build up the insurance fund.

* * *

Chief Examiner of Titles. Originally, this office functioned as counsel to the registrar and as an administrative resource for the county court in matters in-volving land registration. However, over the years, the office has gradually assumed many quasi-judicial responsibilities because of the specialized expertise required and the credibility of the office among local real-estate professionals. Most of the 1966 legislative revisions were developed by this office.

The chief examiner is an experienced real estate attorney appointed by the chief judge of the county court on the basis of recommendations of the inde-pendent screening board. The staff consists of five additional people: two experienced attorneys, a law clerk, and two secretaries. The 1977 budget is $135,000 for personnel, supplies, and equipment. Administratively, the office is part of the county judicial system. The chief examiner reports directly to the chief judge of the county court.

Under the law, the chief examiner has three major functions: (1) to examine the title status of land under application for registration and advise the court on registration matters; (2) to act in a judicial capacity in a variety of situations requiring authorization of corrections or amendments to certificates and of the replacement of lost certificates; and (3) to serve as legal counsel to the registrar.

* * *

The responsibilities described are similar under the statutes of the three states. The major difference is in Massachusetts where the three-judge land court retains judicial functions assigned to the chief examiner in the other jurisdictions. However, the land court's examiner plays a role almost identical to the other chief examiners in his capacity as an advisor to the judges. Here again, the size of the Franklin staff and the budget required is based on the experience of the existing systems.

* * *

Lincoln's 1966 legislative revisions require that the chief examiner's office be operated on a self-sustaining basis. Meeting this requirement has been problematic, since a major responsibility of the office involves advising the registrar. As a result, the 1976 adjustments to the registrar's fee schedule included the imposition of a $15 charge at the time of each transfer of ownership of registered land. The current 1977 projection of 4,300 transfers of registered land is expected to generate $64,500, which will be collected by the registrar and paid to the chief examiner.

* * *

None of the existing systems uses a fee schedule that accounts for the services provided by the chief examiner. The lack of user income for this office is a major source of deficits requiring subsidies. Consistent with the assumed decision to operate the program on a self-sustaining basis we have attempted to create a fee schedule approximating the requirements placed on this small but important office. Apportioning the cost of supporting the registrar evenly against each newly registered owner seems to be an equitable approach.

* * *

In instances of new applications for registration, the chief examiner serves as an independent investigator of the status of title. Petitioners accompany the application for registration with an abstract of the title history. The chief examiner analyzes that abstract, gathers and examines other evidence relevant to title, identifies persons who may have a possible interest in the application, prepares a report on these matters for the court, and generally supervises the movement of applications through the judicial process. The fee for this service is $300. It is expected that the 100 registration applications projected for 1977 will yield $30,000 in revenues.

* * *

Historically, assisting the court in processing applications for registration and examining the title histories to the land involved was the primary function of the chief examiner. Over the course of time, two major changes have occurred. First, as the respective systems matured, judges have increasingly relied on the advice and opinions of the examiner. Second, as the volume of new applications has diminished, more and more of the examiner's time is required to address the problems arising from land already registered.

To search the title history on registration applications, the Massachusetts Land Court appoints an examiner from a list of qualified practicing attorneys who are not employees of the court. This practice is similar to the procedure used in the smaller counties in Minnesota, where the volume of applications is too small to justify a full-time position. The efforts of private attorneys contribute to making registration costs higher in Massachusetts than in the other states. While the practice undoubtedly holds forth the promise of an independent review, it seems to be an exercise in undue caution. We assume, therefore, that there is no need for establishing this requirement in our hypothetical state of Lincoln.

There is no existing correlative to the $300 fee for the services provided by the chief examiner during the Franklin registration process. The closest analogy is the $150 charge imposed by the Massachusetts Land Court. This charge is in addition to the $400 to $600 estimated cost for the services of the independent attorney-examiner appointed by the land court. In contrast, there is no examiner's registration charge in the two urban Minnesota counties, and the Cook County registrar imposes only a $30 charge (but see note on page 6).

The lack of income from services provided initial registrations is another source of the deficits in the existing programs, which are subsidized from other revenues. The $300 charge we assume for the Franklin chief examiner is necessary to prevent comparable deficits. It is calculated to reflect an average workload of two professional person-days per application.

* * *

The third major service provided by the chief examiner involves the conduct of proceedings requiring the alteration of certificates to conform to changes in circumstances. Such changes include a variety of fact patterns involving transformations in the legal status of registered owners, amendments to trust documents, and the death of registered owners and related probate situations. They also include the correction or deletion of erroneous or obsolete memorials, covenants, and other restrictions appearing on certificates and the replacement of lost owner's duplicates. In 1977, it is estimated that the Franklin chief examiner will conduct approximately 650 proceedings of this kind.

Under Lincoln's initial Torrens legislation, most such proceedings were conducted in court. Since many of them proved fairly routine, the 1966 legislative revisions shifted responsibility for them to the chief examiner in order to streamline disposition of recurring problems arising in the certificate system. On the average, each of these proceedings requires from one to three hours of a professional staff person's time. Accordingly, a fee of $50 is assessed by the office for each proceeding. Such fees are expected to generate $32,500 in 1977.

* * *

Assumption of the responsibility for corrective proceedings of the kind described in the text represents one of the major historical developments in the function of the Torrens chief examiner. Each of the existing systems shows a course of evolution along these lines over the last twenty years in order to minimize the use of judicial resources for fairly routine matters. Since most of the matters involved in these proceedings result in changes to certificates that are dispositive of vested property interests, the responsibility is best described as judicial in character.

The 650 proceedings estimated for the Franklin office represent a ratio of between one and one and a quarter percent of the number of registered land parcels in the system. This is the approximate percentage of parcels requiring proceedings of this kind in the existing urban systems. As before, the fixed fee is assumed to keep the program on a self-sustaining basis.

* * *

The County Court. The primary role of the court under the current Lincoln statute is to conduct proceedings and issue decrees for new registrations. In practice, the chief examiner's investigation of title status constitutes most of the effort required for the preparation of a decree. However, in about 15 percent of the cases, a hearing is required because of the need to assess witness testimony or because an intervening or opposing party contests some aspect of the application. On the basis of the experience of prior years, it is estimated that approximately fifty to sixty judge-days will be required to entertain the 100 registration applications expected in 1977.

In addition, it is expected that the court will be required to hear something in the neighborhood of sixty to seventy cases involving problems with registered land, which cannot be disposed of in proceedings conducted by the chief examiner. These cases involve problems unique to the Torrens system and are to be distinguished from foreclosures, tax takings, and other legal proceedings that routinely arise in cases of registered and unregistered land alike.

* * *

The text reasonably describes the involvement of the judiciary in registered land matters in the jurisdictions we examined. The Massachusetts Land Court presents an exception because of its unique involvement in the statewide administrative apparatus. In all other respects, experience shows a decline in the magnitude of the role played by the judiciary in Torrens systems generally and a commensurate increase in the administrative and quasi-judicial responsibilities of the registrar and the chief examiner.

* * *

The court fee for registrations and other cases involving registered land is $25. This is the same amount charged for court cases generally. The Lincoln Torrens legislative requirement for cost-of-service user charges does not apply to court fees.

The Insurance Fund

In 1963, the Franklin Torrens insurance fund held approximately $110,000. Up to that time, there had been few successful claims against the fund. However, a series of claims in 1964 and 1965 reduced the balance to below $30,000. The impact of this rash of claims led to the 1966 legislative revisions.

The revisions abandoned as inequitable the original approach of obtaining contributions to the fund only upon initial registration and upon the transfer resulting from the death of a registered owner. The new law continues to require a contribution at the time of initial registration. However, the amount required has been adjusted upward by replacing the original formula (one-tenth of one percent of the assessed value of the property) with a new one: $50, plus one-quarter of one percent of the assessed value. In addition, the new law requires the sum of $10 to be paid the registrar for the insurance fund at the time of each subsequent transfer of registered property. This additional assessment is based on the theory that every transfer of registered land contributes to an increase in the risk of error, exposing the fund to the liability, and that each new owner should bear some part of the cost of the fund.

* * *

The small size of the Franklin insurance fund—$110,000 in 1963—is consistent with the experience in all American Torrens jurisdictions except for Cook

County. The low frequency of valid claims is also consistent with the experience of the existing urban programs. The sudden appearance of substantial claims in the mid-sixties is, of course, a fiction we created to illustrate certain problems.

Both Minnesota and Cook County have made recent changes in the fee schedule aimed at increasing the size of the fund and spreading the cost in part to current owners. The approach described for Franklin is drawn in part from these experiences.

* * *

This new fee structure has substantially replenished Franklin's Torrens indemnity fund. At the close of 1976, its total stood in the amount of $750,000, including almost $40,000 in income earned from investment in government securities that year. In 1977, it is estimated that the registrar will collect $43,000 from transfer fees and the chief examiner will collect another $27,000 in charges from initial registration applications.

Since 1966, approximately $70,000 has been paid from the fund. This entire amount was paid on claims arising from errors that had occurred prior to 1966. There have been no claims brought on the basis of events occurring since.

During the formulation of the 1966 revisions, there was considerable debate in the legislature over the extent of coverage that should be provided from the fund. As the result of a compromise, the law currently specifies that the maximum amount payable on a specific claim is the assessed value of the property at the time of the most recent payment into the fund. Further, attorney's fees and other costs sustained by a claimant in defending his property and in prosecuting a claim against the fund are specifically excluded as recoverable damages. However, the statute charges the chief examiner with the responsibility of assisting claimants in the assertion and defense of their registration rights.

Administratively, the fund is managed by the county treasurer under the direction of the chief judge of the county court. Investment is restricted by law to government securities, and the fund is subject to a biennial audit by the state auditor. It is specifically stated in the law that the legislature intends the fund to be self-sustaining, and that neither the county nor the state are to be liable for claims in the event of fund depletion.

* * *

The 1966 Lincoln revisions with respect to fund coverage illustrate problems that remain unresolved under the statutes governing existing Torrens systems. Basing maximum recovery on the assessed value at the time of initial registration is a common practice. The reluctance of a legislature to increase the exposure of a limited fund is understandable. Although Lincoln's new maximum is based on assessed value at the time of the most recent transfer, this maximum is still inadequate, considering the recent inflation of real-property values and the common practice of assessing real property below market value.

Lincoln's denial of indemnification coverage for legal and other expenses associated with a claim, and its disclaimer of any additional state or county responsibility for fund inadequacy, is consistent with the policies of other Torrens insurance funds. Again, the legislature's interest in minimizing liability exposure is understandable. Constraints on recovery undoubtedly discourage the pursuit of claims. However, this works a seemingly unjustified hardship on landowners and investors, many of whom have no choice but to accept registration status established by prior owners.

* * *

New Registrations

New registration applications in Franklin have averaged approximately 100 annually over the last five years. The overall history shows a marked tendency toward diminishing numbers of new applications. This is commensurate with population stabilization and a decline in the rate of property development. In peak years—in the early 1920s and again around 1960—new registration applications exceeded 1,000 per year.

The primary objective of new registrants is to cure defects in title history. Tax forfeitures during the depression have given rise to problems that are still being presented for resolution. In addition, redevelopment efforts in older parts of the core city are creating circumstances well suited for disposition by the conclusiveness of the registration decree. Franklin lawyers are reluctant to rely on the boundary-line determinations produced by the somewhat imprecise surveying techniques relied upon in earlier generations. As land values have risen, they feel that the cost of securing registration is worth the value of eliminating doubts that may arise from an ambiguous history, even when there is no specific defect or question presented. This frequently arises where a project involves piecing together several smaller parcels, each of which has a singular history of ownership and development.

The persons most likely to seek registration continue to be builders, developers, and other promoters of land-improvement ventures for commercial purposes. Use by speculators anxious to enhance the marketability of undeveloped property is not as common as it once was. Homeowners are also rarely involved in new registration applications. While some current applications involve land planned for residential development, this use pattern shows signs of a steady decline that is consistent with population stabilization. The most frequent residentially related application for initial registration involves the conversion of apartments and other structures to condominiums.

* * *

The described use pattern for new registrations is similar to that of the jurisdictions examined. Except in Cook County, where new registrations have almost ceased, there is a clear pattern of diminishing use. Beginning around the mid-1960s, the decline in applications for new registrations has been steady but gradual. The decline appears to be attributable to several factors: the need for registration is diminishing, since land with obvious title defects has already been identified and the defects cured by registration or other means; there is little land left with ambiguous title histories (usually undeveloped and held within the same family for many years); and suburban expansion and related development is slowing.

* * *

The 1966 revisions requiring that operational costs be fully sustained by users have had a substantial effect on the cost of obtaining new registration. As summarized in table 2-1, the current cost of obtaining initial registration for property assessed at a value of $100,000 is approximately $1,265 compared with a cost of approximately $500 in 1966. This amount is an estimated minimum only. The history of a particular land parcel might dictate higher abstracting costs and legal expenses and may require a survey. As a general rule, the time required to process a typical application for initial registration is about seven to eight months.

There is no evidence to suggest that the increased cost of obtaining registration has contributed to the declining use described earlier. Since registration is most frequently used by commercial interests either to facilitate the marketability of land or to enhance its commercial value in connection with improvements, the expense involved is viewed as a normal cost of business. The expense is hardly great enough to deter the use of registration where circumstances make its use desirable.

* * *

The $1,265 estimated expense to obtain initial registration in Franklin is substantially higher than the $550 to $750 average that prevails in the Chicago and Twin Cities areas. The difference is largely due to the fee structure established in Franklin in order to price services on a fully costed basis. Even at that, the Franklin cost is still less than that incurred in Massachusetts today. However, the high Massachusetts expense is attributable to certain unique features—mandatory boundary registration and the use of independent examiners of title—which we assumed were not needed in the Franklin Torrens system.

* * *

Table 2-1
Initial Registration Costs in Franklin (1977)

Court fee	$ 25
Chief examiner fee	300
Abstract preparation[a]	60
Notice, publication[a]	50
Registrar (for certificate)	30
Insurance fund contribution	300
Legal assistance[a]	500
Total cost[a]	$1,265

[a]Minimum estimated cost, subject to upward variance.

Impact on Homeowners

The primary effect of the 1966 Torrens revisions on residential owners of Franklin's registered land has been to increase closing costs required at the time of transfer. The $90 in registrar's charges for the filing and processing of new ownership is $65 more than the $25 required to record a comparable unregistered transaction with the recorder of deeds.

There is an offset against this $65 increase in expense in the form of a possible saving in the amount of approximately $20 to $30 in lower search or abstracting costs. If the abstract is prepared independently by a private attorney, this saving is seldom realized, since attorneys typically charge on the basis of the entire search-and-examination process without distinguishing the two functions. If the abstract is prepared by a commercial abstract company, the saving over the cost for an equivalent parcel of unregistered land is commonly in the neighborhood of $20 to $30.

There is, however, no appreciable difference between an attorney's fee for examining registered residential property and his or her charge for examining an abstract of comparable unregistered property. Attorneys in Franklin generally use an hourly rate for real-estate work, subject to a minimum, which is the fee most frequently incurred in cases of moderately priced housing. In a fairly typical residential transfer—a $50,000 purchase involving a $40,000 mortgage— the customary fee for unregistered land is approximately $225: approximately $50 for the commercial abstract and $175 for the professional service involved. If the property is registered, the fee is typically around $200. The difference is due to the lower cost of abstracting. However, if the lawyer prepares the abstract independently (which is becoming increasingly less frequent), the fee is usually $225 for both registered and unregistered land alike.

Where moderately priced housing is involved, the legal and abstracting costs for search and examination generally arise as a result of a mortgage lender's requirement. An attorney is designated by the lender, and the cost described is passed through to the buyer at the time of closing. If the buyer obtains private legal representation, the expense will again typically be the same for both registered and unregistered property. The buyer also pays the $90 in registrar's charges for the necessary filing and processing of the transfer. The effect is that the buyer of registered residential property typically pays $35 to $40 more than the buyer of comparable unregistered property for the title-related aspect of closing costs.

If title insurance is obtained—which is not infrequent in the Franklin area— closing costs are the same for both types of property. Further, where private insurance coverage is involved, it will be acquired for reasons that apply to registered and unregistered property alike. There are few instances where comprehensive risk coverage is sought for unregistered residential property but not for comparable registered property. In sum, the buyer of insured residential registered property ends up paying $65 more in closing costs than the buyer of comparable unregistered property because of the higher public filing and registration costs.

* * *

As suggested in the text, analysis of the title-related aspects of closing costs by land registration requires careful attention to the different cost components involved, that is, abstracting or search, examination, insurance for risk coverage, and public filing and processing. In a typical case involving residential property, it is in the search component that the Torrens approach offers the potential for a saving in effort and expense. However, this saving is small, generally in the range of $20 to $30, since it represents less than an hour in expended effort. In the systems studied, this economy appears to be realized in only a minority of residential transfers. Even when realized, this saving may be offset by higher administrative filing and processing charges, depending on the amount of the subsidy provided for operating each Torrens program.

The described effect on closing costs is based on the current experience in the jurisdictions examined and is discussed more fully in the following chapter. The comparison provided in the text assumes property that has already been registered by a prior owner. The cost of obtaining initial registration must also be considered in evaluating the full economic impact of Torrens.

3 Evaluation of Torrens

Examination of the Torrens systems in operation in Cook County, Illinois, in Massachusetts, and in Hennepin and Ramsey Counties, Minnesota, enabled us to identify characteristics fundamental to the Torrens approach in the United States. These observations, in turn, were supplemented by information in the literature concerning various attempts at Torrens in the other states and on the concept of land registration generally. Unlike the experience in Great Britain and in some of the English territories, land registration was never compulsory in the United States. Where Torrens was implemented, it was always on the basis of the voluntary decision of individual landowners. Since choice was available, the resulting experience provides important information, including reasons why land registration is sought; landowner objectives being fulfilled; and the kind of land most frequently involved. It also provides a framework of real-life land status situations that enables a realistic evaluation of economic impacts and other circumstances relative to the Torrens alternative.

The Torrens experience in the United States has not been favorable. Its failures are many and its successes are few in number and limited in scope. The systems in operation in Massachusetts and in the Twin Cities are and have been well respected for the relief they afford in correcting unmarketable titles. However, this respect is based on a legal capacity to deal with a set of land-title-related problems (and a human capacity to realize the legal potential) that is relatively narrow in application. Thus, the few Torrens programs that have succeeded continue to function primarily for special purposes.

None of the Torrens systems established in the American states has evolved into one of general-purpose use. The reasons for this are many and varied and are not a function of specific statutory language or imperfections in draftsmanship. Initial registration is expensive for the average landowner, even with a subsidized operation. In addition, the administrative program required to manage registered land is both expensive to operate and susceptible to mismanagement and abuse. Further, even under the best of circumstances, the Torrens approach has certain limitations and problems that are unavoidable. Given these shortcomings, it is understandable why landowners have opted for land registration only in circumstances where a clearly discernible benefit was present—usually in the form of alleviation of problems with the title to a particular land parcel.

Some recent advocates of Torrens theorize the presence of a generalized societal benefit in the form of across-the-board reductions in closing costs for routine transfers of residential housing. This appears to be a modern version of the concerns that found Torrens attractive generations ago. Of course, the end-point realization is considerably different. In the latter part of the nineteenth century, home ownership was far less widespread than today. The audience that was attracted to the untried Torrens consisted of speculators, builders, and investors. Considering the rapidity with which industrialization was expanding the cities, it seems that the time required to perfect titles for transfer was then as important a factor as the out-of-pocket expenses required.

The early Torrens proponents believed that the principal risks in title defects were attributable to a combination of inadequacies in the recording system and the intricacies (often feudal in origin) of substantive real-property law. They felt that adoption of Torrens for the establishment and transfer of ownership interests would indirectly reform the substantive law and that the device of the certificate would fill the voids in the recording system. As a result, Torrens was expected to reduce the amount of expensive and time-consuming legal and other assistance required in real-estate transactions. The only risks perceived were felt to be adequately covered by the existence of the public insurance fund.

Subsequent experience shows that these expectations have not been realized. This, in itself, should be a lesson for the modern Torrens proponents. In his 1938 study, Professor Powell concluded that Torrens could not produce broad-based benefits unless the substantive law of real property was substantially (almost fundamentally) reformed. At that time, the 1925 British reforms (abolishing many feudal real-property concepts and establishing country-wide compulsory registration) may have appeared attractive. The experience over the last forty years has undercut Powell's hopes. Title-related closing costs—in both time and expense—run proportionally higher in Great Britain than in the United States. Despite substantive and procedural "reforms," title searches must still be performed and the resulting histories examined.

The experience in the United States is comparable. The expected widespread benefit from Torrens has not been realized. We found that even with taxpayer subsidy, little, if any, savings in closing costs are being realized in the urban areas with viable Torrens systems. In fact, it frequently happens that title-related closing costs for the transfer of registered residential property are greater than those for comparable unregistered property.

Uses of Torrens

A striking aspect of the Torrens experience in the American states is the failure of any system to evolve into one of general-purpose use. Where Torrens was implemented, it was (and is) used by landowners for special purposes only, primarily to cure unmarketable titles. Other common objectives include boundary clarification, simplification of complex title arrangements involving multiple land parcels, and protection against adverse possession.

Because of differences in the individual histories of the jurisdictions that have attempted land registration, it is difficult to generalize about all user patterns. It is clear, however, from the urban systems we examined, and from the literature available on other jurisdictions, that land registration was and is sought for reasons peculiar to the particular land involved. The predominant reason is to clarify an ambiguity or resolve a potential conflict over the status of title or ownership. Specifically, registration is used to eliminate problems or resolve doubts that would render land unmarketable. This purpose is more than just predominant. It is so overwhelmingly the justification for the use of Torrens as to be its American *raison d'être*.

In this regard, the prime attribute of the Torrens approach is the extent to which the initial registration decree eliminates unrecorded prior history as a consideration that affects land title. Because of constitutional, statutory, and judicially imposed exceptions, a registration decree is not legally conclusive as to all possible claims and interests in the land. However, it is sufficiently exhaustive in its coverage to offer the potential to resolve or eliminate a great many of the problems associated with "bad" or unclear title histories.

The fact that title clarification is the primary reason for using Torrens helps to describe the nature of the land being placed into registration and the motivation of the landowners involved. Historically, much of the land that went into registration was undeveloped or relatively undeveloped and the reason for seeking registration was to enable its sale for (or after) development. This continues to be the pattern in Massachusetts, where the statewide jurisdiction of the land court includes currently developing semirural areas. In built-up urban areas, some current use of registration is more oriented toward the transfer of property for redevelopment. Thus, the primary category of Torrens users includes landowners who stand to enjoy the enhancement of value occasioned by development opportunities—speculators, developers, and builders. This was particularly true during periods of rapid urban growth early in the century.

This historical need for an efficient title resolution mechanism to facilitate urban development is best illustrated in Cook County, Illinois. The impetus for the creation of Torrens there was the great Chicago fire in 1871, which destroyed the courthouse and all public land records. Extensive growth of the urban area in the last quarter of the nineteenth century led to the creation of the first Torrens system in the United States. The city of Chicago grew from a population of 30,000 in 1850 to 1.7 million in 1900 to over 3 million in 1930. Growth of this magnitude required investment in constantly increasing numbers of land parcels that had little or no establishable title histories but were experiencing rapid increases in value. The resulting use of Torrens to resolve unclear titles was extensive up through the late 1920s, making the Cook County system the largest land-registration system in the country. Initial registrations declined rapidly thereafter, because of the diminishing legal significance of the lack of pre-1871 records, and are rarely sought today. A similar history—a fire that destroyed the Barnstable County (Cape Cod) land records in the late 1850s—contributed to making Barnstable County one of the major areas for the use of land registration in Massachusetts.

Title-history clarification and resolution are achieved in most, perhaps all, states today by what are generally referred to as "quiet-title" proceedings, so named because they provide the mechanism to "quiet" the legal meaning of circumstances clouding the efficacy of a given title. In Boston and the Twin Cities, we found a strong preference for registration over quiet-title proceedings, although the two were considered relatively equal in cost and effort, because of the greater breadth in coverage of Torrens and its continued applicability into the future. In Cook County, the opinion of lawyers is to the contrary. Since Torrens in Illinois exists in the one county only, the state law authorizes several quiet-title-type options that Cook County lawyers find more attractive for the resolution of title problems than Torrens.

This leads us to believe that the quiet-title alternative is sufficiently well developed in other states to preclude the need for the creation of a Torrens system today. Thus, the primary need fulfilled by Torrens in Massachusetts, in the Twin Cities area, and in an earlier period of Cook County's history, is probably being met elsewhere by other legal mechanisms fashioned over the years to respond to similar problems. Moreover, it seems likely that the history of urban growth in most cities has already isolated those land parcels most in need of the resolution of poor or defective title histories.

Another reason for the use of Torrens is boundary clarification. For the most part, this applies primarily in Massachusetts because of a history of poorly defined colonial-based titles. However, boundary resolution is also an objective of some current land-registration applications in the Twin Cities area. The reasons for this application are associated with the history of surveying (and the technologies involved) and the early settlement patterns in each of these areas. Thus, it is difficult to generalize about the extent of the need being met by this function. It is clear, however, that this is an important attribute of the registration system in Massachusetts, since boundary determination is required in all cases.

Torrens has also been used as legal protection against adverse possession (sometimes referred to as "squatter's rights"), or the opportunity recognized in law generally—but denied by Torrens—to establish an interest in land by an extended period of continued use. It is reported that owners of large tracts of land sought registration early in the century to protect against this kind of encroachment. This involved mineral holdings in the area of Duluth, Minnesota; timberland in the eastern Carolinas and in Georgia; and large estate and agricultural holdings in Hawaii.

After title-problem resolution, boundary-line determination, and protection from adverse possession, the reasons why landowners seek land registration are considerably varied, making it difficult to list and describe them in full. For example, in real-estate ventures involving the piecing of several parcels of land together—for example, shopping centers and industrial parks—there is always the risk of a minute, but significant, boundary-line gap in the assembly process, which registration can overcome. In addition, registration offers a small advantage in paperwork simplification, through the aggregation in a multi-parcel venture of a great many legal papers pertaining to ownership into a single registration decree and certificate.

Further, in revitalization efforts directed at older areas in the core-city environment, there is some current interest in seeking registration to protect against possible boundary discrepancies arising from surveying techniques relied upon in prior generations, which are less precise than those available today. For these and other reasons, the land for many major office buildings in downtown Boston, Minneapolis, and St. Paul has been registered. Again, Cook County is the exception. There is hardly any registered land within "the Loop" in Chicago, probably because the postfire reconstruction had already reestablished clear title histories in the commercial downtown area before the Torrens system was established.

Analysis of the different reasons for land registration yields the conclusion that the primary users and beneficiaries of Torrens are landowners or investors in land who seek commercial gain. In theory, any landowner might experience a problem in title-history or boundary-line determination that would make registration desirable. In practice, however, neither homeowners nor governmental bodies are common initiators of registration applications. This is primarily because of the lack of any particular benefit to be realized from obtaining registration. For example, clear title histories and boundary lines are typically established before residential housing is built.

This is not to say that registered land is used only for commercial or industrial property. To the contrary, a significant (but unknown) percentage of the registered parcels in each of the jurisdictions examined is the current site of residential housing. The clear historical pattern is for speculators, developers, and others interested in residential development to obtain registration for one of the reasons discussed earlier, or, as frequently happens today, to acquire land for development that is already registered. Thus, there has been a tendency in recent years in Massachusetts and in the Twin Cities area of Minnesota for the location of new registrations to follow the course of suburban sprawl. In Cook County, however, this process stopped well over a decade ago.

Because of the lack of available data, we were not able to quantify the precise number of registered parcels in each of the jurisdictions examined. Comparisons of the numbers of registered to unregistered transfers over recent years suggest that the approximate ratio of registered to total land parcels is between 18 percent and 20 percent in both Suffolk County, Massachusetts, and Cook County, Illinois, about 35 percent in Hennepin County, Minnesota, and about 40 percent in Ramsey County, Minnesota. Current initial registrations in all systems are substantially below the peak volumes reached many years ago and demonstrate a pattern of general decline. This suggests that Torrens applications may be approaching near-maximum levels in the different urban areas—a process that was apparently reached in Cook County many years ago—and that system resources will become increasingly devoted to the administration of land that is already registered.

Limitations and Problems

As indicated in the prior section, the Torrens approach has been used in American states to fulfill certain special needs only. The current use and respect for the systems in the Twin Cities of Minnesota and in Massachusetts demonstrate the viability of the concept in areas where needs of this kind are continuing, although generally declining in overall significance. It seems obvious, however, that the objectives being fulfilled are of limited application only. Even the best of the American Torrens systems have failed to evolve or mature into general-purpose programs for land ownership and record keeping.

The reasons why Torrens has remained so limited in America are many. Land registration is expensive to operate and maintain—for the landowner, for other interested parties, and for the general public. In addition, there are problems and risks associated with Torrens that do not arise under the conventional approach to land ownership and transfer. In short, there are trade-offs that must be made, costs that must be paid to obtain the benefits of land registration. The experience shows that these are trade-offs that landowners have not been willing to make in the absence of special circumstances impairing the value of the property.

The Expense of Initial Registration

In the jurisdictions we examined, a typical uncontested application for land registration costs, in Cook County, $575 to $750; in the Twin Cities area, $555 to $750; and in Massachusetts, $1,500 to $2,000. In each instance, a major part of the cost, as well as the reported variations, stems from the need for legal assistance. The substantial increase in cost in Massachusetts is due to requirements that are not imposed by the other systems, that is, surveying and the use of an independent title examiner.

In Cook County and in the Twin Cities area, the process usually requires an average of six to eight months. In Massachusetts, the amount of time involved is between one year and eighteen months, because of the additional requirements imposed.

The figures cited are minimums, not averages. Although the cost and time involved are not usually greatly affected by either the amount or value of the land, they do tend to increase with the complexity of the title history in question. Moreover, the estimates given are for uncontested applications only. Occasionally, registration applications will be opposed. Where defendants appear to assert or protect their interests, the application process assumes the character of adversary litigation. This contributes to an increase in cost and time commensurate with the legal assistance and other services necessary for resolution of legal or factual disputes.

The expense required to secure land registration appears great enough to discourage large-scale use of the system. Unless a particular problem exists in the title history that will prevent or discourage marketability, registration offers no identifiable benefit for the average landowner, particularly the homeowner. Thus, there is no particular incentive to bear the expense of obtaining initial registration—a fact substantiated by the low incidence of homeowner applications.

The Expense of Administration; Subsidized Operations

At its roots, Torrens requires that all claims and interests applicable to a given land parcel (other than those excepted by statute or judicial decision) be reflected on a single controlling certificate. This basic principle demands an administrative operation of a quality necessary to maintain the integrity of the certificate-based system.

Viewed in functional terms, this essential aspect of Torrens involves the shifting of some of the responsibility for the accuracy and dependability of title history away from the individual efforts of parties to a transaction toward a centralized administrative operation. Under the conventional approach to land ownership, the public office functions much as a library, maintaining little more than copies of documents and one or more indexes that enhance access to the records. In contrast, a Torrens office exercises quasi-judicial functions. Legal documents must be interpreted, and seemingly clerical acts related to the entry of descriptive information onto certificates become dispositive of the legal effectiveness of interests. The original documents must be surrendered by their owners and retained in the registrar's office.

Thus, quality management—manifested in exacting administrative control of day-to-day routine functions—is essential for a successful Torrens operation. The failure to realize this fact was a contributing factor to the lack of success of many Torrens systems around the country. In California, this was perhaps the major factor leading to a lack of use in several county systems and the bankruptcy of the statewide insurance fund. Professor Powell found evidence of similar maladministration in the New York City area in the 1930s. His observation that American jurisdictions seem to be unable to produce the effective civil-service delivery systems of many European nations is largely based on reactions to the slipshod administration he discovered in New York.

We were able to observe the impacts of this need for quality administration in our own examination. In Massachusetts and in Hennepin and Ramsey Counties in Minnesota, we found the land-registration system to be well respected and regularly utilized when needed. However, real-estate practitioners in the Twin Cities area did not feel the same about systems in operation in some other Minnesota counties. Moreover, the numerous complaints we discovered in Cook County appear to evidence an erosion of the credibility of Torrens to the point where the incidence of new registrations has come to a virtual halt.

The practical effect of the Torrens need for quality administration is to require both greater numbers of staff and a higher degree of professional and managerial talent than conventional recording systems. For example, exclusive of judges and administrators, the staffs in Cook County and in Massachusetts include ten lawyers each. Further, because of the degree of care needed and the extra number of documents involved, Torrens requires between two and three times the number of administrative personnel as conventional recording requires to handle the same number of transactions.

In turn, these increased personnel requirements produce operational costs that are considerably higher than those for conventional recording. One result of this additional cost is a public fee structure for processing of registered land documents that runs from 50 percent to over 200 percent higher than that for conventional recording.

Despite the higher fee structure, none of the systems we examined are economically self-sustaining. To avoid deficits, each needs additional revenues in the form of either a direct general appropriation or the utilization of excess revenues from the conventional recording system. While there are considerable variances among the data-reporting formats used by the different systems examined, we estimate that the 1976 "subsidy" ranged from $140,000 in Ramsey County to a high of $625,000 for the statewide Massachusetts program. It is important to note that, owing to the commercial emphasis among primary users of land registration, the subsidy takes on a regressive character, a transfer of income to the wealthier segments of society. Elimination of the subsidy necessarily entails an increase in the filing and other fees charged to users of the registered land system.

The Lack of Conclusiveness of the Certificate

In all jurisdictions, the enabling Torrens legislation contains specified exceptions to the general principle that legally cognizable interests in land must be reflected on the official certificate and substantiated by documents on file with the public office in order to be effective. (See, for example, figure 2-1, which includes the extract from the Massachusetts General Laws that appears on every Massachusetts Torrens certificate.) Further, subsequent judicial opinions have carved out additional exceptions—sometimes on narrow but important grounds, sometimes to prevent an inequity that might arise from the strict application of Torrens principles to a specific set of facts. In cases where these exceptions arise, the interest of a Torrens purchaser or investor is subordinate to the excepted claim or interest.

While there are some variances among the exceptions recognized by the jurisdictions we examined, each jurisdiction recognizes claims or interests arising as follows:

1. From appellate processes pertaining to the initial registration decree. This includes the right to appellate review of a person who was not a party to the actual registration proceeding. Persons who properly should have been made a party enjoy appellate rights beyond normal statutory review periods.
2. Under federal law or the U.S. Constitution, including tax liens, claims and interests from bankruptcy proceedings, and claims raised by Indian tribes under federal law.
3. From current local and municipal taxes and special assessments.
4. From rights of a party in possession of the property, for example, pursuant to a short-term lease (under three years in Minnesota, five in Illinois, and seven in Massachusetts).

Another important exception arising from other real property legislation is for interests in land which are commonly referred to as mechanic's liens. These grow out of claims for payment for work performed and/or materials supplied in improvements—usually construction—to land. Typically, a claimant is entitled to a lien for the period (for example, 90 or 120 days) between the time he was entitled to be paid and that required for the official recording or registration of the claim. In Minnesota, it is settled that the mechanic's lien attaches to registered land during this short period even though the lien has not been filed and entered on the certificate. In Illinois and in Massachusetts the issue is unresolved, a fact that gives rise to a presumption in practice that a mechanic's lien is valid during its brief prefiling period and must be protected against.

As a practical matter, the significance of these different exceptions is that prospective purchasers and investors cannot rely entirely on the Torrens certificate for assurance as to unencumbered ownership or the priority of a security interest. This means that evaluation of title status necessarily involves a search for information that is located off the certificate (and outside the registrar's office) and may be impossible to find. Thus, purchasers and investors must resort to the same methods of title assurance commonly used for unregistered land. For example, in transactions involving new construction, where the potential for sizable mechanic's liens is great, this assurance is frequently obtained through title insurance.

In other instances, the purchaser or investor needs assurances as to possible bankruptcies, federal tax claims, and unpaid local taxes and special assessments that might affect the land involved. In Cook County, the registrar provides two special tax searches, one for IRS liens and another for local taxes and assessments. Assurance for other excepted claims and interests is sometimes obtained from title insurance. In the Twin Cities area, where commercial abstracting is an essential part of real-estate practice, information relative to some of the excepted claims and interests is reported in a special form of abstract used for Torrens property. In Massachusetts, where neither title insurance nor commercial abstracting is prevalent, an attorney retained for title examination and certification searches for exception-type information independently.

In recent years, a special application of the common exception for federally based claims has arisen in the form of claims of different Indian tribes to substantial land holdings. To the extent that an otherwise meritorious claim of this kind is based exclusively on federal law, it will probably prevail against registered land. In Massachusetts, where litigation of this kind is presently pending, we encountered much concern about this particular exception to the coverage of the land court's certification.

Special Landowner Risks and Expenses

Ownership by Fraud. The essential feature of the Torrens approach--that the validity of ownership and the existence of other nonexcepted real-property interests is determined by the offical certificate—can produce some unfamiliar and sometimes costly circumstances for the registered landowner. Perhaps the most startling example of this arises from the extent to which the concept of the certificate can work to divest the interest of an otherwise lawful owner in favor of an innocent purchaser.

The legislation in each of the jurisdictions we examined provides that a purchaser of registered land taking a certificate of title for value and in good faith holds the title subject only to the excepted interests and the interests noted on the certificate at the time of transfer. In addition, each statute contains provisions specifying that the certificate is conclusive evidence of the matters contained therein. Each of these provisions is fundamental to the Torrens approach.

The effect is to create a situation whereby an innocent purchaser, P, can acquire legally valid title from F, in whose name the current certificate reflects the ownership interest, even though that certificate had, in fact, been obtained by a forgery of a transfer from O, the original registered owner of property. (See *Eliason* v. *Wilborn* 281 U.S. 457 (1930).) Under conventional real-property law, *O* would retain the ownership interest on the principle that *F* had no valid interest to convey to *P*. Thus, by assigning the paper certificate the function of serving as the exclusive determinant of ownership interests, the Torrens approach works to shift the accepted allocation of risk of loss in the event of forgery or other fraud. Under Torrens, this is a risk that a registered owner must bear, even though there is no realistic opportunity to prevent a fraud or forgery from occurring.

Misfiled Interests. The central role that the official certificate plays in the disposition of property interests creates still other risks for the unknowing landowner. Since the maintenance of the certificate lies exclusively under the control of the public administration, there is always the possibility that a properly filed mortgage, judgment, or other lien or interest in the property can be entered on the wrong certificate without the knowledge of the affected parties or the opportunity to prevent it from happening.

Suppose, for example, that a mortgage given by *A* on property owned at 21 Elm Street was, in fact, memorialized on *B*'s certificate for the property at 22 Elm Street. Neither *A* nor *B*, nor *A*'s mortgagee, are normally in a position to know of this error, which may continue uncorrected for years. This leaves *A* in a position to sell the property free and clear of the mortgage, since it is not memorialized on the certificate. *A*, of course, remains liable on the promissory note secured by the mortgage, but that debt may be impossible to collect once the property is sold. Meanwhile, *B*, who has no personal liability on the note or mortgage, will be unable to sell the 22 Elm Street property (or to obtain a mortgage thereon) until the improper entry is removed. This may be done administratively or it may require court action, since the statutes involved show great reluctance to entrust the Torrens administration with the discretion to alter or amend even erroneously prepared certificates.

Circumstances such as those described, along with others of a similar nature, have arisen in the jurisdictions we examined. For the most part, they have been rare. Their significance lies in the fact that they *can* happen because of the inherent dependence of the Torrens approach on the existence and accuracy of entries on a single piece of paper. The effect is to place the landowner in a position of potential jeopardy from administrative errors and mishaps over which there is no personal control. The effect is also to require the more expensive and higher quality administrative staff discussed earlier.

Of course, the Torrens insurance fund is available to compensate persons for some damages of the type described. A mortgagee, for example, might be able to recover for the loss resulting from a misfiled mortgage. However, the compensation available might not be considered adequate to the homeowner defrauded out of his or her property. Nor will compensation be awarded for the nuisance associated with the bureaucratic hassles and out-of-pocket expenses (for legal assistance) that may be required to get an erroneous certificate corrected or for the delay and expense (because of funds held in escrow) required before a transaction can be consummated.

Amending Certificates; Replacing Duplicates. The dominant position occupied by the certificate under the Torrens approach is the source of still another kind of problem that potentially can beset any registered homeowner. The primary device relied upon to prevent the kind of fraudulent abuse just discussed is an owner's duplicate certificate issued to the owner at the time a certificate is prepared. In order for the property to be legally transferred, that is, a certificate prepared in the name of a new owner, this duplicate *must* be surrendered to the Torrens office along with a deed from the registered owner.

Duplicates are frequently lost or mislaid, however. This expands the vulnerability of the owner to fraud. It also poses a frequently recurring problem in that a new duplicate *must* be obtained before a legal transfer of ownership can occur. Each of the systems we examined has a special proceeding for the issuance of new duplicates. This is a quasi-judicial function, not a simple administrative matter, since care must be taken that the duplicate goes to a proper owner only. In Massachusetts, a petition to the land court is required. And, while legal representation is not required, the majority of cases of this type in Massachusetts and in the Twin Cities are handled by private lawyers. A further expense is involved in the form of necessary public fees: $41 in Minnesota; $35 in Cook County; only $5 in Massachusetts.

A similar kind of proceeding is required in just about any kind of situation, short of an actual voluntary transfer, involving a change in ownership name or status from that attested to by the official certificate. This can range from a simple change in the owner's legal name to several different types of situations arising from the death of one or more of the registered owners. Divorces, as well as changes in partnership or corporate status or in trustee-beneficiary relationships, present the same problem. Since a transfer of registered property can be accomplished only by a deed signed by the persons indicated as owners on the certificate, certain quasi-judicial proceedings must be available to validate changes to the certificate needed to conform to the changes in ownership circumstances.

In addition to changes in ownership status, a proceeding is also necessary to amend certificates, to correct or remove matter that was erroneously entered or is legally obsolete or ineffective. For the most part, the proceedings required to handle these different matters are substantially routine and consist of the examination and confirmation of legal documents attesting to the circumstances supporting the change to the certificate. Some may require witness testimony. Except in Massachusetts, where land court approval is always required, most of these proceedings are administrative in nature. There are occasional instances where court action may be necessary. Whether handled administratively or judicially, the subject matter is essentially legal, and in well over the majority of cases the landowner will be bearing the expense of a minimum of two to four hours of legal assistance, plus related registrar fees for preparing the new certificate. Finally, we note that proceedings of this type are by no means rare. The experience of the systems we examined indicates that they occur on a ratio of between 1 and 1.5 percent of the number of land parcels in registration annually. That is, there will be between 1,000 and 1,500 proceedings of this type each year for every 100,000 registered parcels of land.

Inadequate Insurance Funds

All Torrens systems authorized in the United States required the creation of an insurance fund—established by assessments of fees (originally one-tenth of one percent of the value of the land) collected at the time of the application for initial registration and at the time of transfer at the death of a registered owner—to compensate persons for damages sustained as a result of the administration of the system. Except in Massachusetts, which confines fund coverage to losses occurring after initial registration, indemnification is available for property interests that were improperly cut off at the time of the initial registration decree.

The funds are relatively small considering the amount of land involved. As of the end of 1976, the $4.6 million Cook County fund is the only one of significant size. The funds for Massachusetts and for Hennepin and Ramsey Counties in Minnesota amounted to $346,000, $248,000, and $98,000, respectively.

In part, the meagerness of the funds and the infrequency of successful claims may reflect the highly circumscribed coverage afforded by the Torrens certification. In the jurisdictions we examined, successful claims against the fund have been few. However, concern for the size of the funds is not unjustified considering the history of Torrens in other jurisdictions. The bankruptcy of the California statewide fund played a major role in the repeal of Torrens in that state. A similar experience in Nebraska earlier in the century contributed to the cessation of further use of Torrens in that part of the country. In this regard, it is important to note that a major source of potential liability lies with the day-to-day administration of Torrens records rather than the initial judicial registration process. Substantial claims can arise from simple clerical errors, for example, in typing the legal description of the property on a new certificate or in failing to enter properly filed interest on the right certificate.

Independent of the small size of the Torrens funds, there are several troublesome unknowns as to the nature and extent of the coverage involved. One unknown directly related to the size of the funds arises from a lack of certainty over the extent, if any, that other governmental assets are available to compensate for fund inadequacy. Another arises from implications in the appropriate statutory language (except in Cook County) that a claimant must go to court to establish liability against the fund. This may make sense from the standpoint of assuring that a public fund is properly administered. However, it discourages expeditious settlement of deserving claims and may discourage the pursuit of smaller claims. It is possible, for example, that the burden of litigation, together with legal uncertainties, has helped to keep the number of actual claims small over the years.

It is not clear in any of the jurisdictions whether the compensation available includes the legal and related expenses associated with the defense of one's interest and the prosecution of a claim against the fund. Finally, there is no clear resolution for the ages-old insurance debate over the standards of valuation to be used to measure recovery maximums. There can be, for example, substantial variance between the market value of the property at the time of a loss and its assessed value at that time or the assessed value at the time the first payment was made into the fund.

Uncertainties such as those briefly summarized here, together with the actual smallness of the funds, has substantially undercut the indemnification feature of the Torrens approach. As a result, landowners and other investors in land generally seek mechanisms for assurance of title to registered property, including commercial title insurance coverage, which are identical to those used for unregistered property.

Torrens and Homeowner Closing Costs

General Observations

As a general rule, only about 10 percent of total residential closing costs are affected by circumstances related to title status. Expenses for services related to the exchange between buyer and seller (for example, for sales commissions, for taxes, and for contract and deed preparation) and for services related to the obtaining of a loan by the buyer (for example, credit reports, appraisals, mortgage preparation, and loan commitment or origination fees) account for approximately 90 percent of closing costs and are not affected in any way by the title status of the land involved. It is only in the narrow category of title-related services—expenses incurred for assurance of good title, that is, search, examination and certification or insurance of title, and the necessary public fees for recording or filing—where the registered status of land produces some differences in the procedures utilized.

We found that the existence of registered or Torrens land produces little or no opportunity for the realization of a significant saving in title-related closing costs in typical residential transactions. The term *net saving* refers to the potential for total title-related costs, the sum of required public filing charges[a] and other title-related expenses, to be lower for registered property than for property of comparable value that is not registered.

In the Boston area, the net title-related costs in a routine transfer involving registered residential property tend to run slightly higher ($13) than those for comparable unregistered property. In the Twin Cities area the common pattern is for closing costs to be slightly lower ($11). In the Chicago area, registered residential property can generate a net saving of approximately $100. However, in about 25 percent of Cook County transfers, this saving will not be realized and the title-related costs for the closing of typical registered residential property will exceed those for comparable unregistered property by at least $75.

If clearance measures are in order, that is, if steps are necessary to resolve a problem disclosed by search and examination, the possibility for Torrens to deliver a reduction in the efforts and expense required is directly dependent on the nature of the problem involved and the possible adversity of opposing interests. In some instances, Torrens might require a judicial or quasi-judicial administrative proceeding that would not be needed for unregistered land. In others, Torrens might provide a more expeditious remedy. In still others, the effort required might be substantially the same as for unregistered land.

We found that much the same holds true with respect to commercial transactions. Commercial and industrial properties involve such a wide range of diversity and degree of complexity that it is impossible to generalize as to the economic impact of Torrens at transfer. Thus, we confined our inquiry into closing costs to "typical" residential transactions only, that is, those involving a seller with an unpaid mortgage balance who had purchased the home within the last ten years or so, a buyer with a new mortgage, and no particular title problem requiring clearance measures.

How Title-Related Closing Costs Are Incurred

The title-related aspects of closing costs consist of three distinct components: services required for search and examination of title history; insurance (or risk assumption) coverage, if obtained; and filing or registration fees required by the appropriate public office. While there are significant variances in the customs and practices commonly followed among the jurisdictions examined, we found that the existence of registered land occasioned little in the way of economic

---

[a]Public filing charges are those currently assessed. We do not include the cost of services supported by a subsidy from general tax revenues. See the section of this chapter headed *The Expense of Administration; Subsidized Operations.*

differences with respect to each component. This is the case whether or not title insurance is purchased. The use of title insurance for registered land is discussed in the next section. It should be noted here, however, that title insurance services frequently involve the search and examination component together with risk assumption coverage.

Typically, title-related residential closing costs are incurred at two levels. The first type is nondiscretionary insofar as the seller and buyer are concerned and consists of expenses incurred by the seller pursuant to his or her legal obligation with respect to producing good title. This obligation is imposed by the purchase-and-sale agreement and usually follows the custom in the area. Nondiscretionary costs also include expenses for services required by mortgage lenders in order to assure the validity and priority of the collateral interest taken in the land to secure the loan. These latter costs pass directly through to the buyer, whereas the former may or may not. For purposes of examining the impact of Torrens on title-related costs we focused on the services and costs involved without attempting to differentiate between buyer and seller absorption.

The second type of title-related costs consists of those which a buyer might incur by choice. These expenditures might be for efforts that duplicate or are in addition to those already undertaken at the insistence of mortgage lenders. For example, a buyer might seek a title insurance policy that is separate and distinct from that issued to the benefit of the lender. Or, legal advice as to title status may be sought independent of that made available to the mortgage lender. The attorneys interviewed reported an increase in recent years in the frequency of home-buyer legal representation. This is probably because of recent increases in the cost of housing. For this reason, we included both discretionary and non-discretionary costs in our examination of the impacts of the Torrens process.

Registration and Filing Fees

In all jurisdictions examined, the Torrens filing fees typically incurred for residential transfers are higher than those for unregistered land. In Massachusetts and in Minnesota, the dollar amount is not great, the additional cost being at least $9 and $13 respectively, for residential property. If the subsidies involved in these operations were eliminated, the additional cost would be greater. In Cook County, where the attempt is being made to place registration fees on a cost-of-service basis, the additional cost for the Torrens transfer is between $46 and $98. This means that the closing costs for Torrens land will always be higher than for unregistered land unless an equivalent or larger saving is generated in another cost component.

Search and Examination

The major component of title-related closing costs grows out of the expenses incurred for search, examination, and certification of title. In the jurisdictions examined, we found that a different one of the three commonly accepted methods for title search and examination was the prevailing practice:

> In the Boston area, private attorneys are regularly used for both search and examination.
>
> In the Twin Cities area, the prevailing practice is the attorney-abstract method, wherein private attorneys examine commercially prepared abstracts.
>
> In Cook County, title insurance has displaced both commercial abstracting and the efforts of private attorneys and is used almost exclusively.

In Boston and in the Twin Cities, mortgage lenders require a certification or opinion of title by a private attorney or firm. Registered land is subject to this requirement along with unregistered land. In either case, the tasks performed and the methodologies pursued by the attorneys are similar. That is, a search must be undertaken that involves verification of the seller's ownership interest, identification of any terms or conditions that may qualify the ownership interest, and identification of other claims and interests that may also be outstanding against the property. Some of this information is obtainable by examination of the registration certificate and the supporting documents on file with the registrar. However, information relative to the status of current taxes and special assessments is located in other public offices, and information relative to federal tax liens and bankruptcy proceedings may be located in still another office.

On the average, the efforts required to perform the search necessary to disclose the information relative to title status are somewhat less when registered property is involved. Because of the aggregation of many of the interests in the property on the single certificate, there is a convenience in the search function that may result in a saving of time. However, this saving in the case of typical residential property must be measured in minutes, not hours.

This is best illustrated in the practice in the Twin Cities area, where searches are performed through the vehicle of commercially prepared abstracts. In that area, the price for the continuation (update) of a registered property abstract for typical residential property ($25 to $30) is approximately $20 to $25 cheaper than that ($50) for an abstract for comparable unregistered property. This differential is an adequate economic expression of the efficiencies potentially available from the Torrens approach—the equivalent of less than an hour of a professional's time. However, it seems that the streamlining of high-volume specialized abstracting is required to produce even this small economy. We were not able to find a comparable saving under the Boston practice, where attorneys perform the search themselves or supervise its conduct.

Examination of Title

In Boston, and frequently in the Twin Cities area, the examination of title will be performed by private attorneys to meet the requirements of the mortgage lender. This results in a written opinion or certification of title status provided by the attorney. As indicated earlier, this applies for registered and unregistered land alike. In the Boston area, this opinion is rendered for the legal benefit of both the lender and buyer. In the Twin Cities area, the attorney's opinion typically extends to the lender's interest only.

In both areas, there are some variances in the pricing approaches used by the different attorneys and firms whose practice includes search and examination of resident property for mortgage lenders. However, no cost differentiation is generally made that admits to a distinction in level of effort between registered and unregistered property. In typical residential transactions, the fee for property of comparable value is the same. The law firms involved report the use of hourly billing rates for real-property work. However, the rates involved are typically subject to a minimum for routine residential work, which is computed by either a flat rate or on the basis of a percentage of the mortgage (or purchase price) or some combination of the two. Under any of the approaches used, the legal fee for typical residential property will be the same whether the property is registered or not.

The result in the Twin Cities area is a small saving in closing costs in favor of the transaction involving registered property. With the identical attorney's fee for examination and opinion of title, $9 in additional charges for public filing and processing services, and an approximate $20 to $25 saving in abstracting, the title-related closing costs for typical registered residential property in urban Minnesota are $11 to $14 cheaper than those for comparable unregistered property. In general, somewhat the opposite is true in the Boston area. There, the attorney's fee for the combined search and examination effort is the same. Combined with the extra public charges, the registered residential transaction ends up costing $13 more.

In Cook County, there is an opportunity for the Torrens residential transaction to produce title-related closing costs as much as $100 lower than those for nonregistered property of the same value. In this area the only comparison that can be made has to be on the basis of either the presence or absence of title insurance, since the prevailing custom does not admit to the use of either the attorney or the attorney-abstract method for title assurance. The saving exists because some mortgage lenders in the area do not require title insurance in many cases where registered land is involved, whereas title insurance will almost always be required for unregistered property. (This practice is discussed more fully in the following section.) These lenders require a limited "sketch" survey for uninsured registered land, a service performed in all cases but included in the cost of title insurance, but they do not impose any additional fees for the examination of the Torrens certificate and related indexes. This latter examination is typically performed by staff personnel rather than by outside attorneys and amounts to a stage in internal processing that is not required for unregistered land.

However, in approximately 25 percent of the registered transactions in Cook County, title insurance is required by mortgage lenders. In these cases, the title-related closing costs for Torrens residential transactions will be higher than for unregistered property, since the insurance will cost the same and the public filing charges can be as much as $98 higher.

If an uninsured Torrens buyer in Cook County—that is, a buyer of registered residential land whose lender does not require title insurance—elects to retain personal legal representation, the saving in closing costs is potentially eliminated by that part of the fee involved which is attributable to title search and examination. This function is not undertaken by private attorneys if title insurance is involved (for either registered or unregistered property), since the custom in the area is to rely on the assurances of the title company. The practical effect is that where buyer legal representation is involved, the saving over title insurance for the typical Torrens transaction can be reduced to something below $50 and may not be realized at all.

In the Boston and Twin Cities areas we found that both kinds of property incurred similar costs when the homeowner seeks personal legal assistance. In both areas we found some variety in the legal services sought by home buyers and the opportunity that may exist for fee negotiation. However, the feeling among lawyers and others interviewed was unanimous to the effect that the legal fee for "typical" homebuyer representation was commonly the same for comparable registered and unregistered property.

Caveats

It should be noted that the discussion in this section is concerned with a comparison of title-related closing costs involving the transfer of property that is already registered and being administratively maintained pursuant to a subsidized Torrens system. In our judgment, the elimination of the subsidy can only work in the direction of making the closing costs for registered residential property greater than those for unregistered land. Further, given the current expense for obtaining initial registration (discussed in the prior section), the closing costs for property that is registered as a condition of transfer, will, of course, be significantly higher than those for unregistered land.

Finally, the cost of initial registration must be taken into account in assessing the true total cost involved in those cases where a potential net savings can be realized from Torrens. For example, the possible $100 saving we found in Cook County is well below the present value of benefit obtainable by the $550 to $750 investment required to seek and obtain registration. This explains why residential property is placed into registration by homeowners only in the case of compelling circumstances related to the particular land involved. We would not expect a homeowner to make a minimum $550 investment where the maximum measurable benefit was no greater than a potential $100 saving that could be passed to a buyer at some uncertain time in the future.

Torrens and Title Insurance

There is an unfortunate tendency in some of the Torrens literature to treat land registration and private title insurance as mutually exclusive concepts. This tendency is (or, more properly, *was*) perhaps understandable since the establishment of an insurance fund for damage indemnification is a central feature of land registration. However, it fails to take account of the fact that the Torrens insurance coverage is fairly narrow in scope and that private title insurance includes a range of risk coverage and a set of transaction-related services that are in addition to indemnification for title-related losses.

In the areas with ongoing Torrens systems, we found that title insurance is acquired for registered land with a frequency that closely approximates its use for unregistered land. As a general rule, the decision to acquire title insurance is unrelated to the registered status of the land involved. That is, the reasons that support the decision to obtain insurance apply, for the most part, with equal force whether land is or is not registered. Thus, all other circumstances being equal, residential Torrens property is about as likely today to be the subject of title insurance as is comparable unregistered land. We also found that the charge for the insurance (which frequently includes other land-transfer-related services) is the same for either land-status category.

The only exception to these findings demonstrates the differences between private title insurance and Torrens, in terms of both risk coverage and transaction-related services, and underscores the impossibility of treating the two as generally substitutable for one another. In Cook County, title insurance is the predominant mechanism relied upon for title assurance in real-property transfers. However, some mortgage lenders, particularly suburban institutions, do exempt registered land from their otherwise universal requirement for title insurance for residential properties. This exemption is not a general one; nor does it free the Torrens transfer from expenses for services, which are not required if title insurance is obtained. For example, a survey will be required. Further, whenever the lender is in doubt about the status of the title from a review of the Torrens certificate or whenever any one of a number of conditions apply—including new construction or possible sale of the mortgage on the secondary market—these institutions require title insurance. This behavior indicates a perception of private insurance as a broader product, with Torrens acceptable as a substitute only for properties considered after examination to be presumptively risk-free and when supplemented by the additional assurance provided by a survey of the property. These institutions do not obtain the protection deemed necessary for their own interests on the basis of the Torrens law alone.

In regard to the use of title insurance, it is important to note the differences in practice that exist among the three jurisdictions. The Boston area, which had the highest title-related costs of the jurisdictions we examined, makes very little use of title insurance. While commonly used for new housing developments and for other commercial ventures, title insurance is seldom utilized in the transfer of existing residential housing. The major mechanism utilized for title assurance in the Boston area is the opinion of title rendered by private attorneys.

In contrast, as noted earlier, the medium of title insurance is used almost exclusively in the Chicago area—for search and examination of title in addition to risk underwriting. The practice for residential transfers in the Twin Cities area falls somewhere between the extremes represented by the Boston and the Chicago customs. There, in some cases, title insurance is used for risk coverage only and is written on the basis of a private attorney's opinion of title. In other cases in the Twin Cities area, title insurance displaces the efforts of abstractors and private attorneys and includes the search-and-examination function as well. In both the Chicago and the Twin Cities areas, title insurance includes a range of transaction facilitation services in addition to matters of title accuracy and completeness.

This comparison illustrates the danger in using the term *title insurance* without defining the range of services involved in any given case. We found that the nature of the private insurance product varies, depending on the custom and practices of the area. Analysis of the differing practices among the areas also highlights the fallacy of attempting to compare title insurance with land registration. Two entirely different products are involved. The nature of the public product is fixed by statute, whereas the private offering varies depending on circumstances and needs of individual parties. The experience in the major Torrens jurisdictions shows that the two play complementary roles with respect to title-related problems and are not in practice substitutes for one another. For example, in Massachusetts, it is not infrequent that title insurance companies refer prospective clients to the land court to cure uninsurable titles.

Torrens and title insurance differ substantially in terms of the extent of the promise of indemnification against future losses, that is, the conventional meaning attributed to insurance. As discussed in the second section of this chapter, both statutes and judicial decisions have carved out exceptions to the Torrens coverage that involve certain commonly recurring claims and interests that threaten the completeness of a land title. In addition, there is always the risk of additional exceptions being imposed by later judicial decisions. One practical effect of the various exceptions is to exclude any loss resulting from their realization from the coverage of the Torrens insurance fund.

The potential losses resulting from claims and interests excepted from the Torrens certificate will vary in any given transaction. However, their sum total is sufficiently great to encourage mortgage lenders and other investors to obtain the risk-underwriting coverage of title insurance for registered land. Of course, some of the expected risks are of more significance than others, with respect to both their frequency of occurrence and the extent of the potential loss that might result. For example, the possibility of mechanic's liens and arrearages in taxes regularly encourages lenders to seek title insurance where new construction is involved. Federal tax liens and other federal claims (for example, those arising from bankruptcy proceedings) are also common where construction is involved.

Further, a demand for private insurance for registered land continues to exist because of the small amounts of money in the Torrens funds and because of certain limitations and legal uncertainties over the extent of fund coverage. As discussed earlier in this chapter, the statewide fund in Massachusetts had approximately $350,000 and the Minnesota funds in Hennepin County and Ramsey County had approximately $150,000 and $100,000 respectively, as of year-end 1976. These amounts are surprisingly small, considering the amount of land involved. For example, a single Hennepin County claim, which was reported in 1977 to be properly payable in the sum of approximately $20,000 amounted to over 13 percent of a fund accumulated over seventy years.

Historically, the actual claims paid by the systems we examined have been few. This may be a reflection of the limited coverage provided by the Torrens approach, aggravated somewhat by limitations on recovery (discussed later) that discourage pursuit of a claim. However, as with any risk factor affected by human performance, major investors demonstrate concern over future potential, not just past experience. Other Torrens systems have failed because of bankrupt funds. From this point of view, even the Cook County fund, with close to $5 million, is not very large.

In addition to preferring larger insurance funds, investors also seek private insurance to cover deficiencies in the amount of compensation available from a Torrens fund on a particular claim. The Minnesota statute limits recovery from the fund to the value of the property at the time of initial registration or the most recent payment into the fund. The other statutes are silent on the point, inviting a similar interpretation, since initial registration and transfer upon the death of a subsequent registered owner are the major events that give rise to a contribution into the fund. This may mean that, for the majority of the land registered in each jurisdiction, the maximum recovery for any particular parcel was established before 1930. The inflation of property values in the last five years alone is persuasive of the need for more comprehensive indemnification coverage. Further, the Torrens statutory provisions deny compensation for expenses directly connected with defending against an attack on registered property interests. They also (except in Cook County) appear to require court action to perfect a claim. This discourages private settlement and increases the range of noncompensable damages.

Still another set of reasons reported to us for obtaining title insurance for registered and unregistered land alike derives from the particular interest of mortgage lenders. By law and/or practice, lenders must obtain a security interest in land that is not only legally valid but also has priority over all other interests except for that of the owner. The Torrens approach assures that the security interest is recognized if it is properly memorialized on the certificate. However, it does not assure the priority of that interest vis-à-vis other valid interests that might or might not appear on the certificate. Nor does it assure that the loan itself is valid and enforceable. To obtain indemnification coverage assuring both priority and enforceability, residential lenders, particularly investors in the secondary market, look to private insurance.

A final consideration underlying the use of title insurance for both registered and unregistered land is the ability of title companies to provide a wide range of services related to the facilitation of timely and effective execution of real-estate transactions. This is an intangible, often described to us by practicing attorneys and lenders as the ability and willingness "to make things come out right," which is separate and apart from both search-and-examination services and risk-assumption coverage. This feature of the private insurance product contributes to its utilization for both registered and unregistered land. Above and beyond the framework of its legalistic coverage, the title insurance product includes services aimed at successfully cementing the instant transaction and resolving problems that may arise in the process. Most of these activities are unrelated to questions of title *per se*, and are, therefore, outside the scope of the Torrens certificate.

Thus, for a variety of risk-related reasons—some directly concerned with title, others with transactional problems—owners, lenders, and others with interests in registered land continue to seek title insurance for the same services and risk coverage they seek for unregistered land. Despite the differences in custom in the jurisdictions we examined, the practices were similar in practical result. With few exceptions, the decision to obtain private insurance is based on considerations unrelated to whether the land involved is or is not registered. In terms of closing costs, the economic effect is to place the transfer of registered land in the position of having the same title-assurance costs as for comparable unregistered land, in addition to the extra administrative costs for the registration system.

4 The Twin Cities

Introduction and Background

Introduction

The initial statute providing for the registration of land titles in Minnesota was enacted in 1901. It was substantially amended, indeed replaced, in 1905 as part of a general revision of the public statutes. This subsequent enactment—together with amendments—constitutes the present law as reported in Chapter 508 of the Minnesota Statutes Annotated (MSA). The statute is preceded in the MSA volume by an extensive note, written by R.G. and Carroll Patton (both of whom were Torrens officials in Hennepin County), which is recommended for its comprehensive analysis of the subject matter.

Originally, the Minnesota Torrens law applied only to counties with a population in excess of 75,000 persons. As a practical matter, this meant only Hennepin (Minneapolis), Ramsey (St. Paul), and St. Louis (Duluth) counties. However, a 1909 amendment made registration permissible in all other counties.

Today, most Minnesota counties maintain a system for Torrens registration. The three original urban counties, along with Anoka County, which was added in 1953, are unique, however, in that they maintain a full-time Office of Chief Examiner of Titles; in the others, the examiner is appointed by the court and compensated by the individual registration applicant. As a result, land registration in Minnesota, although authorized and controlled by a uniform statute and set of judicial opinions, amounts to a series of individual county systems.

We examined the operations of Torrens in the twin cities of Minneapolis and St. Paul—Hennepin and Ramsey Counties, respectively. Because of geographical proximity and the standardizing influences of influential legal academicians (serving as Torrens examiners as well as commentators), prominent real-estate practitioners and areawide mortgage lending, abstracting, title insuring, and other business interests concerned with land, there is considerable identity between the two. In virtually all important respects, the twin city/county areas represent or combine to form the core of what is a single metropolitan area. Whether looked at individually or jointly, they contain the highest percentage of registered land in any urban area in the country.

Local Real-Estate Customs and Practices

As the result of long-established custom and habit, the Twin Cities area can be accurately described as devoted to the attorney-abstract method for search and examination of real-estate titles.

Pursuant to the attorney-abstract approach, an abstract of title history is prepared or brought up to date at the request of a party to a transaction. In the case of residential property, the custom in the area is that the seller orders the abstract and bears the cost of preparation or continuation. Several companies in the area are regularly engaged in providing abstracting services.

The up-to-date abstract will be delivered to an attorney, typically the attorney for the buyer's lender, who will examine the abstracted entries and issue an opinion, or certification, of title based on the contents therein. This certification relates to matters of record only. It does not cover questions covering the security of boundaries, the existence of unrecorded but valid mechanic's liens, municipal special assessments, and so forth.

If title insurance is desired, which is common in the Twin Cities area, the insurance might be written on the basis of the attorney's written opinion. Or, since most title insurance companies doing business in the area are also engaged in the abstracting business, the title company might be retained to handle the entire process. That is, the company will bring the abstract up to date, have it examined by its own attorneys, and issue the policy in a single integrated operation.

The attorney-abstract method for the performance of the basic search-and-examination function for land transfers is, of course, followed in many parts of the country. However, it is so deeply embedded in the habits and customs of parties involved with real estate in the Twin Cities area as to have affected basic terminology. Nonregistered land in this area is regularly referred to as "abstract" property in order to connote a distinction from registered or Torrens property.

This does not mean that registered land is not the subject of abstracts. To the contrary, registered property abstracts (RPAs) are routinely utilized as the basic vehicle for examining the title to registered property.

One might ask—as we were prone to do—why the RPA? By virtue of the mechanics of Torrens, the certificate performs many of the same functions as an abstract, since it portrays essential information as to interests that affect title status. The answer is twofold. First, the RPA provides information on interests relevant to title that are excepted from Torrens coverage and could not, therefore, be reflected on the certificate of title, for example, bankruptcy and federal liens. Second, abstracting costs are sufficiently low to make it uneconomic for a law office to attempt to establish procedures to gather and assemble this information itself. For example, while the cost of bringing an abstract up to date varies, dependent on the entries required, the going rate for a typical abstract for residential property is $45 to $50. RPAs are slightly cheaper; $25 to $30 is a fairly standard charge at the present time.

The custom in the Twin Cities area is for the seller of property to bear the cost of bringing the abstract up to date. The seller may also bear the costs of clearing defects revealed by the examination. All other costs arising from title search, examination, and insurance are borne by the buyer.

The Torrens Operation

General Description

Minnesota's enactment retains all the essential features common to the American versions of the Torrens model. An applicant seeking registration obtains a judicial decree to that effect. The decree declares fee-simple title subject to interests and encumbrances judicially recognized as of the time of registration. The decree binds all persons, known or unknown, whose interests may have been adverse. The law allows for the certification of boundaries as well as of title, but this aspect of the procedure is currently used in only 5 to 10 percent of the cases.[a]

As a result of the registration decree, a certificate is prepared in the name of the owner. A duplicate certificate is issued to the owner, and the master certificate remains on file with the county registrar of titles, who is also the county recorder for conventional deeds. Voluntary transfers of title are achieved by deed, which must be accompanied by the transferor's owner's duplicate.

Subsequent claims or interests in the land must be filed with the registrar in order to have any legal effect against the land. This includes obvious interests in land, such as mortgages, as well as general money judgment liens and attachments. However, it does not include mechanic's liens for work performed or materials supplied within the last ninety days.

The general Minnesota law provides that mechanic's liens in land are valid against third parties if recorded within ninety days after the completion of the work or the furnishing of the material giving rise to the claim on which the lien is based. The case of *Armstrong* v. *Lally*, 209 Minn. 373 (1941), held that this applies to registered land. Thus, the situation is created wherein a purchaser (or any other person claiming an interest in the land) could find his or her interest being subject to a mechanic's lien that was not recorded on the certificate at the time of purchase, but was subsequently filed and recorded within the statutory time period.

---

[a]This is probably due to the earlier history of extensive surveying in this part of the country by the federal government. In 1818, that part of Minnesota which lies east of the Mississippi River was made a part of the Michigan Territory—an area surveyed pursuant to the rectangular system established by the Northwest Ordinance of 1787. Minnesota was organized as a territory in 1849 and admitted as a state in 1858.

In addition, certain statutory exemptions (discussed later) provide the basis for other claims and interests, which can be valid against the land without being entered on the certificate. Subject to these exemptions, a bona fide purchaser or other claimant of an interest in registered land is legally entitled to rely on the certificate as conclusive evidence of the legal status of the title.

An assurance fund created by payments assessed against users of the registration system is maintained for purposes of indemnifying losses occasioned by the operation of the system, for example, an interest that was terminated because of a failure of recognition at the time of the initial registration decree or an otherwise valid interest that was not properly memorialized on the certificate.

Exceptions

As suggested earlier, the protective features of the Minnesota Torrens system are not available to cover all conceivable claims and interests in real property. MSA Section 508.25 provides certain exceptions, which qualify the conclusiveness of the registration decree and the subsequently prepared certificate. These are:

1. Interests arising or existing under federal laws or the Constitution;
2. The lien of any tax or special assessment for which the land has not been sold at the date of the certificate of title;
3. A lease for a period not exceeding three years pursuant to which there is actual occupation of the premises;
4. Rights in public highways;
5. Rights to appear, contest, and appeal the registration application as provided in the established procedures; and
6. Rights of any party in possession under deed or contract for deed from an owner of a certificate.

In addition to these six statutory exceptions, the Minnesota courts have carved out further exceptions over the years. By and large, these judicial exceptions relate to the failure, for one reason or another, to join a proper party at the time of the registration proceedings; for example, a person in actual possession at the time of registration is entitled to remain in possession if not properly joined. The decisions also recognize the power of the courts to go behind a certification to set aside a registration decree because of fraud, to establish boundary lines by "practical location" (that is, on the basis of an agreement, which does not appear on the certificate, established between adjoining landowners in earlier years), or to resolve the conflict between two inconsistent but outstanding certificates. In addition, there is the lack of full coverage of mechanic's liens, discussed earlier.

The practical effect of these exceptions is to dissuade a potential purchaser or lender from relying entirely on the exclusivity of the registration decree and the interests subsequently memorialized on the certificate. If the land in question has been only recently registered, one might be concerned over the proper joinder in the registration proceeding of all persons with an interest in the land and the possibility for a potential appeal. Elapsed time since registration would resolve some of these doubts but could still leave questions over the rights of necessary persons not properly joined, which the courts can recognize beyond the six-month statutory appeal time.

However, there still would be concern over the potential for adverse interests arising from the other exceptions. Thus, a prospective purchaser (or other person seeking a secure interest in the land) would be best advised to inquire into (1) the nature of the interest of any party other than the registered owner who is occupying the premises; (2) the existence of any unpaid taxes or special assessments; (3) claims based on bankruptcy proceedings, tax liens, and other claims by the federal government, or other potential interests in the land based on federal law; (4) the status and existence of adjoining public highways or highways over the premises; and (5) if the boundaries are not registered, the accuracy of the property boundary lines.

Mechanics of Registration

As indicated earlier, initial registration is a function of judicial determination. The proceeding is initiated by the filing by a landowner of an application with the district court. The application is supported by an up-to-date abstract with respect to the property in question. If it is desired that the boundaries be registered, the application is also supported by a completed survey tied in with fixed points. Unlike Massachusetts, boundary registration is permissive in Minnesota, not mandatory. It is sought by landowners today in only 5 to 10 percent of the cases. However, a survey might be needed for the practical purpose of establishing an adequate description of the land. In such a case, record owners and others with an interest in adjoining land will be joined as parties to the proceeding.

After filing, the case is referred by the court to the chief examiner of titles (hereinafter referred to as examiner) who examines the title and files a written report with the court. In Hennepin and Ramsey Counties, the examiner is a duly constituted public office, staffed with experienced real-estate attorneys, and appointed by the district court.

In addition to providing analyses and conclusions as to title, the examiner's report identifies necessary and potential defendants who might have a claim or interest in the land. Legal summons and notice by publication are processed and served in accordance with standard legal procedures. If a defendant elects to contest the matter, the registration is tried like any other civil action, but without a jury. Actual contests over title are rare. However, it is not infrequent that parties enter an appearance to ascertain the impact of the proceeding on their property or to clarify a boundary or right-of-way, or the like.

In the majority of cases, registration applications are uncontested. The applicant still must appear and prove his or her case. In Ramsey County the hearing is before the court; in Hennepin County it is before the examiner, who functions as a referee appointed by the court. The nature of the hearing is dependent on the quality of the applicant's claim to title.

The court makes its determination (or acts on the referee's report) and issues an "order and decree of registration." This is the official judicial act that establishes the title in the name of the applicant. The title will be subject to such interests and encumbrances as are determined valid at that time, as indicated in the decree.

A certified copy of the order and decree is then filed with the registrar of titles, who prepares the certificate of title. A duplicate certificate for the owner is also prepared. In addition, the Minnesota law makes allowance for a mortgagee's and a lessee's duplicate. The initial registration papers remain on file with the court.

Mechanics after Registration

Voluntary Transfers. Subsequent to registration and the preparation of the initial certificate, a transfer of ownership is accomplished by the cancellation by the registrar of the owner's duplicate and the master certificate and the preparation of equivalent documents in the name of the new owner. A transfer can be accomplished only by the voluntary submission of a deed conveying the property accompanied by the surrender of the owner's duplicate and an affidavit of the purchaser, or pursuant to an order of the court or the examiner. If the registered parcel is to be divided, it is necessary for a registered land survey to be submitted to the registrar.

A typical case of voluntary transfer arises from the sale of a residence. This requires the submission to the registrar of (1) the deed conveying the property from the seller to the buyer, (2) the seller's owner's duplicate, (3) a satisfaction of the preexisting mortgage from the seller's mortgagee, and (4) the new mortgage from the buyer's mortgagee.

The new certificate prepared by the registrar will state the ownership interest of the buyer. In addition, the security interest of the buyer's mortgagee will be reflected in a memorial entered upon this certificate, together with any continuing interest, such as an easement. The fact of the prior ownership of the seller and the interest of the prior mortgagee is not shown. The former certificate is cancelled and is retained by the registrar, as are all original documents affecting the property, that is, deeds, mortgages, and so forth.

The registrar's actions in accepting documents, canceling and preparing certificates, and entering memorials thereon amount to considerably more than administrative functions. Under Torrens law, a legal interest in registered property is not valid (for example, a transfer of ownership is not legally effective) until the supporting documents are accepted and acted upon by the registrar. In both Hennepin and Ramsey Counties, the internal processing required takes between two days and two weeks, depending on the volume of activity.

Involuntary Transfers. There are a wide variety of circumstances in which a transfer of ownership arises from situations wherein the registered owner (as reflected by the certificate) is either unable or unwilling to act or where the legal environment is such that the court must compel or oversee the act of transfer. They range from the situation in which the owner lacks the capacity to execute a legal transfer (as in the case of minority or incompetency), to that in which the court compels the transfer (as in the case of a recalcitrant former spouse after divorce or a mortgage or tax foreclosure), to that in which the owner is deceased and the transfer is in accordance with the law relevant to property distribution.

The special procedures needed for the more commonly recurring situations involving involuntary transfers are discussed later. It is sufficient at this point to note that the Minnesota statute, consistent with other American Torrens legislation, denies the authority to the registrar to act in situations such as these. The judgment and discretion required to deal with such situations is entrusted to either the court or, in certain instances, the examiner. The responsibility of the registrar is to act only on their formal instructions, the documentation for which is duly filed and retained in order to perpetuate a traceable chain of relevant interests in the property.

Adverse Interests. Adverse interests include those which are not authorized by the affirmative action of the registered owner. Typically, they do not affect the ownership of the land itself, but constitute a claim or interest against the land directly, as in the case of a mortgage or easement, or indirectly, as in the case of a judgment against the owner, which has the legal effect of becoming a lien against his or her real property. In many instances the adverse claim or interest can ultimately defeat the registered owner's fee interest. Claims and interests such as these include general money judgments, attachments, and mechanic's and other liens. In addition, MSA Section 508.70 authorizes the filing of a notice of adverse claim. This is essentially a catchall designation that subsumes a variety of possible claims of right, title, or interest that are adverse to that of the registered owner(s).

The obligation of the registrar in instances of adverse claims is to satisfy himself that the proffered claim is of a kind that is entitled to be filed and memorialized on the certificate. This requires a degree of professional knowledge and understanding necessary to identify and interpret the proper kind of instruments required to support the claim. The required documentation is filed and retained in order to provide a proper understanding to any person subsequently examining the title. One function of the examiner's office is to provide instructions and guidance to the registrar on these matters.

An adverse claim that is accepted for filing is then memorialized on the master certificate. This does not mean that the claim is valid or automatically defeating of the owner's interest. Consistent with the concept of Torrens, the major purpose of the procedure is to capture the fact of the existence of the claim. If subsequent litigation or negotiations lead to the termination or perfection of the claim, that legal fact will be filed and memorialized as appropriate.

Special Proceedings

As just indicated, the Minnesota Torrens Act requires the use of special proceedings to deal with certain situations affecting interests in registered land. These can be generally described as situations that, because of a need to provide judicial scrutiny or to protect against fraud or abuse, do not lend themselves to treatment by the routine administrative techniques applied to voluntary transfers or the registration of adverse interests. In some instances, the situations that fall in this category are unique to a given set of facts. In others, they recur with some degree of frequency.

Originally, all of the proceedings described here required judicial action and were referred to as "proceedings subsequent." In recent years, however, the Minnesota statute has been amended to allow many of the more regularly recurring proceedings to be conducted by the examiner's office. Thus, the majority of these proceedings are handled administratively today, for the most part on an informal basis and without time delays.

Together, these proceedings provide a substantial part of the statutory responsibilities of the examiner's office. In 1976, the totals were as follows: Hennepin County, 1059; Ramsey County, 372.

Lost Duplicate Certificates. The owner's duplicate certificate must be presented to the registrar in order for a deed to be accepted to accomplish a transfer of the land. An analogous requirement exists for a mortgagee with respect to the mortgagee's duplicate in order to institute foreclosure proceedings. If the duplicate is lost or cannot be located, it must be replaced in the context of a proceeding that assures that the new duplicate is issued to the proper party.

Under a 1976 amendment to the Minnesota Torrens Act, this proceeding can be conducted by the examiner, instead of the court, if all registered owners (or mortgagees, if that is the lost duplicate) sign a statement stating why the duplicate is unavailable. The statement is presented to the examiner, who has the obligation to satisfy himself as to the propriety of the statement. An attorney can appear on behalf of the persons signing the statement.

Once satisfied, the examiner posts a legal notice to the effect that a new duplicate will be issued unless objections are filed within one week of posting. Lacking valid objections, the examiner approves the statement for filing and issues a directive to the registrar to issue a new duplicate. The statement is memorialized on the master certificate of title in order to maintain the descriptive chain of legal events. The registrar's fees for this activity amount to $42. There is no separate examiner's fee.

The authorization for the examiner to conduct the "lost certificate" proceeding was effective April 1, 1976. In the remaining nine months of 1976, the Hennepin County examiner of titles conducted 136 proceedings of this type. This is consistent with an estimated 200 comparable proceedings conducted by the district court in 1975. The Ramsey County examiner does not keep figures by category of special proceedings, but it is estimated that approximately 20 percent, or 44 of the total of 372 administrative proceedings conducted by that office in 1976, were concerned with lost certificates.

Owner's Death: Probate Deeds or Decrees. In the event of the death of a registered owner, a procedure is necessary to honor any resulting transfer of ownership rights. In the case of the death of a joint tenant or a life tenant, the continuing interest of the surviving tenant (typically the spouse) or the remainderman is reflected in the description of ownership interest on the master certificate of title. Thus, the registrar can accept the necessary legal documents and enter appropriate memorials on the certificate without the need for direction from either the examiner or the court. In such cases, a death certificate, appropriate affidavits from the surviving parties, and, in some instances, inheritance tax clearances are the documents required to effect the transfer.

Other than in these situations, the real-property interests of a deceased registered owner will pass either by will or intestate distribution. In 1965, MSA Section 508.69 was amended to authorize the examiner to certify probate deeds and decrees pertaining to a transfer of title to registered land. In such cases, the examiner examines the probate file and related documentation and issues directives to the registrar to enter memorials, prepare new certificates, and so forth, as appropriate.

These proceedings comprise a substantial part of the examiner's quasi-judicial responsibilities. In 1976, the Hennepin County office handled 573 proceedings of this kind, up from 400 in 1975, of a total of 1059 special proceedings.

Divestiture of Owner's Title. This category of special proceedings invests the examiner with the authority to examine and certify (to the registrar) legal documents that award title to persons other than the registered owner. The most common situation involves the divestiture of title as the result of a divorce.

If the parties to a divorce agree as to the disposition of registered land that had been jointly owned, or are willing to abide by a judicial decision, there is no particular problem. The spouses can jointly execute a deed to a new owner or to the spouse who is to take exclusive title to the property. The owner's duplicate is then presented to the registrar along with the deed, and the transfer is processed like any other voluntary transfer.

If, however, the parties cannot agree and the spouse divested from the land ownership interest by judicial decree is unwilling to cooperate in the execution of a deed, then a procedure is necessary to obtain an ownership certificate in the name of the appropriate former spouse.

Under a 1973 amendment to MSA Section 508.59, the examiner has the authority to examine the court file, judgment, and decree for legal sufficiency and issue a directive to the registrar to cancel the existing certificate and prepare a new one in the name of the prevailing party. This is a necessary procedure if the divorce decree does not contain its own directive to the registrar to cancel the existing certificate and issue a new one in the name of the prevailing spouse.

In 1976, the Hennepin County examiner certified 141 proceedings of this kind, up from 120 in 1975.

Directives to Alter Memorials. Occasionally, memorials on certificates reflecting interests on registered land become ineffective by virtue of obsolescence or lack of legal vitality. Pursuant to MSA Section 508.71, the examiner can, upon request, amend or cancel memorials that fall in this category.

As a practical matter, the examiner's activity in this area is concerned with covenants imposing racial restrictions, legal interests barred by statute (for example, judgments that, under Minnesota law, lose their viability as liens after ten years), mechanic's liens by claimants who have failed to pursue the claim within a prescribed statutory period, and other rights that expire by the very terms of the instrument that created them.

In 1976 the Hennepin County examiner issued 75 directives to the registrar to alter or cancel memorials.

Trustee's Deeds. This is a narrow category of special proceeding applicable to situations where trustees—in the context of corporate dissolutions or ordinary trusts, whether or not administered by a court—wish to convey title or other interests affecting registered land. The responsibility of the examiner is to verify the validity of the trust and the power of the trustee to affect ownership interests in the land. Once validated, the examiner certifies the appropriate deeds and instruments to the registrar. In 1976, the Hennepin County examiner certified 64 trustee's deeds.

Proceedings Subsequent. In all situations other than those previously described, and in any of the described cases that involve irregularities, a party wishing to effect a change to property interests reflected by the certificate, or a memorial thereon, must apply to the court for an appropriate disposition. By definition, this procedure applies to a wide variety of situations resulting from a change in circumstances that requires an alteration of the official documentation on record with the registrar. These include situations common to registered and unregistered land, as well as those unique to the Torrens system.

Some common circumstances requiring this kind of judicial procedure include: mortgage foreclosure; ownership resulting from a tax sale; the addition of land resulting from the vacation by a governmental body of an alley, street, or highway; the correction of an error occasioned by a prior registration proceeding or an inappropriate action by the registrar; or a dispute between parties that involves a contention over facts and/or law requiring judicial resolution.

By their nature, proceedings of this kind fall into the category of regular judicial proceedings. They are not rare, however. In 1976, they were involved with the following frequency: Hennepin County, 272; Ramsey County, 150.

Some, perhaps as many as 50, of the 272 proceedings subsequent in Hennepin County in 1976 are attributable to lost duplicate certificates, since the legal change allowing the examiner to handle such matters was effective as of April 1 of that year. This suggests that the volume of judicial proceedings subsequent in both counties should be 15 to 20 percent lower in future years.

The Assurance Fund

Pursuant to the Minnesota statute, a separate assurance fund is required to be created and maintained by each county operating a Torrens system. The purpose of the fund is to compensate persons for losses wrongfully sustained as a result of the administration of the registration processes. This includes property interests improperly cut off or limited by the initial registration decree as well as those adversely affected by subsequent administrative actions.

Fund Administration

The assets in the fund were initially exclusively generated by the imposition of a fee paid by the landowner applicant at the time of initial registration and by the heirs or devisees of the property upon the death of a registered owner. The fee, which is still collected at the time of initial registration, varies depending on the value of the land. It is calculated on the basis of one-tenth of one percent ($1 per $1,000) of the assessed value of the land, excluding improvements. Under Minnesota law, the assessed value of land is computed as a percentage of market value.

Under a 1976 amendment to the Torrens Act, this fee is now supplemented by an additional fee of 50 cents for the entry of each memorial onto a certificate. This amount is paid directly into the assurance fund and, because of the volume of memorials, is expected to generate a substantial increase in the fund size. For example, it is anticipated that the Hennepin County registrar of titles will enter in excess of 40,000 memorials in 1977, generating over $20,000 for the assurance fund in addition to the fees imposed at initial registration.

One reason for this recent change in the funding approach is the seeming inadequacy of Torrens assurance funds in Minnesota. As of the close of 1976, the two funds in the Twin Cities areas stood as follows: Hennepin County, $148,000; Ramsey County, $98,000.

In the event that a fund is insufficient to satisfy claims, the Minnesota statute provides that any unsatisfied balance should be paid from the first sums coming into the fund. Thus, the implication is that neither the general assets nor the full faith and credit of the county or the state stand behind the fund. Considering the large amount of registered land in these two counties, the fact that claims have been virtually nonexistent over the years does not ameliorate the concern that investors, landowners, and others might have about the relatively small amounts in the existing funds.

Claims Management

In both Hennepin and Ramsey Counties, there is no record of a valid claim ever having been presented and paid from either assurance fund. Professor Powell reported in his 1938 study that only one claim had in fact been presented in this area as of that time (in Ramsey County), that it had been denied as unjustified, and that no subsequent litigation had been brought by the claimant.

Since that time there appears to be no evidence of a claim even being presented, except for one that is presently pending in Hennepin County. This claim is apparently valid. It is being brought by a mortgagee whose security interest was inaccurately memorialized on the wrong one of several parcels owned by the same landowner/mortgagor, leaving the parcel that had been mortgaged in a position to be sold free and clear of the mortgagee's interest. The Hennepin chief examiner has evaluated the claim to be worth approximately $20,000 and has recommended to the court that it should be paid from the fund.

The Minnesota Torrens Act provides that any recovery against the fund is limited to the fair market value of the real property as of the time of the last payment into the fund with respect to that property. The Act also states, but does not require, that a claimant "may institute" a court action to recover compensation.

The lack of claims against the assurance fund has precluded the opportunity to resolve some questions that are unanswered by the statute. For example, it is not clear whether it is proper for the county authorities to honor a claim as the result of informal settlement, that is, without the authorization of a court judgment, or in the context of pending litigation. Further, it is unknown whether legal fees and related costs are to be considered the kind of damage that can be compensated for by the fund in the event of a valid claim. Finally, considering the 1976 amendment, which imposed the additional 50-cent fee at the time of an entry of a memorial, there is some uncertainty as to the interpretation to be accorded the preexisting statutory limitation on compensation to the fair market value at the time of the last payment into the fund. The Hennepin chief examiner advises that the statutory maximum of fair market value is now to be computed as of the time of the most recent 50-cent payment applicable to the property in question. However, considering the accelerating value of land in the last few years, together with the fact that the original fee structure for the fund was based on the unimproved value of the land, the uncertainty on this point cannot be considered insignificant.

Economic Considerations

Frequency and Extent of Registration

We commented at the outset of this chapter that the Twin Cities area had the highest percentage of registered land of any U.S. urban area. In fact, precise figures are not available in either county as to the exact number of registered land parcels, or the acreage or value of the land involved. However, it is widely accepted by all parties concerned that an intelligent "guesstimate" places the percentage of registered parcels between 35 and 40 percent for Hennepin County (about 105,000 of approximately 280,000 land parcels) and between 40 and 45 percent in Ramsey County (about 51,000 of approximately 120,000 land parcels).

Analysis of the business records of the offices of the two recorder/registrars suggests that these estimates might be slightly high. For example, as table 4-1 illustrates, the Hennepin County office shows an annual ratio of abstract to

Table 4-1
Hennepin County Deed Volumes

	Abstract	Torrens	Total	Percent Torrens
1974	16,370	7,448	23,818	31.3
1975	18,139	8,663	26,802	32.3
1976	21,550	10,864	32,414	33.5

Torrens deeds presented for filing that is consistently in the neighborhood of two to one. Ramsey County reports data in terms of total documents only, without affording a breakdown as to deeds, mortgages, and so forth. However, examination of those records suggests a percentage of activity for Torrens land that is somewhat less than the 40 to 45 percent "guesstimates."

We are uncertain as to the proper interpretation, if any, that can be drawn from these data. Historically, a good deal of the land that was registered was farm land and other undeveloped property. Land of this kind tends to have a lower turnover rate than urban residential parcels. It is possible, therefore, that annual records reflect what may be considered a minimum expression of the true percentage of Torrens property and that the accepted "guesstimates" are, in fact, fairly reliable. Perhaps the important point is that the frequency of registered land is significant and consists of at least one-third of the land parcels in the combined Twin Cities area.

It is clear that new registrations are continuing to take place, although at a somewhat slower pace than in the past. The data on new registrations in recent years are given in table 4-2.

Historically, registrations were heaviest in the mid-twenties and again in the decade from approximately 1955 through 1965. This demonstrates a pattern of frequency of registration that coincides with new construction and expansion. Note, for example, the substantial decline in 1975 applications as a result of the recent recession.

It is important to point out that the numbers depicted here do not necessarily convey an accurate impression of the numbers of new land parcels going into registration. Because of subparcelling—whether in the form of conventional subdivisions or condominiums—a single application may involve the registration of multiple parcels. For example, one of the 160 applications in Hennepin County in 1976 involved a tract of land broken into 77 parcels. Thus, the

Table 4-2
Applications for Registration, 1970-1976 (Hennepin and Ramsey Counties)

	Hennepin	Ramsey	Total
1970	188	66	254
1971	184	85	269
1972	174	66	240
1973	160	65	225
1974	205	60	265
1975	126	28	154
1976	160	45	205

decline in registration applications over the last decade should not be interpreted as reflecting an absolute decline in terms of actual parcels coming into
registration. Further, since land cannot be withdrawn from registration in
counties containing first-class cities (which includes both Hennepin and Ramsey
Counties), the percentage of registered land continues to grow at a steady,
although gradual, rate.

Cost of Initial Registration

A major consideration for landowners contemplating registration is the cost and
time required to process an application. We found that the cost of initial registration was in the neighborhood of a minimum of $550 to $750 and that the
time required was approximately six to eight months. These estimates are
minimums only and are based on the assumption of uncontested cases and the
absence of a need for boundary registration or clarification. A survey would
involve an additional cost, and legal fees would increase commensurate with
the efforts required to prepare and conduct a contested trial, defend against
an appeal and so forth.

The typical case, however, appears to be one that is uncontested, is relatively uncomplicated in terms of title history, and does not require the conduct of a survey. Within the $550 to $750 estimate of minimum cost, the
largest single component arises from the need for legal services. Legal costs
also involve the greatest degree of variability. The average fees cited to us ranged
from $400 to $600. Typically, these fees reflect efforts undertaken to secure
registration without regard to the amount of land involved or its market value.
Further, there appears to be no difference in this range of customary fees
between Hennepin and Ramsey Counties.

The costs typically incurred in the pursuit of land registration are broken
down in table 4-3. This breakdown shows that the minimum cost of initial
registration will be $553 plus the amount over one dollar that is equal to one-
tenth of one percent of the assessed unimproved value of the land.

Once land is registered, additional cost considerations arise from its registered status. They exist in the form of charges for subsequent transfers and the
filing of related instruments, which are higher than those for nonregistered
land, and in the form of a possible need for the use of one or more of the
special proceedings described earlier. These costs are discussed in the following
section.

Cost of Subsequent Activity and Administration

After land is registered, it remains forever registered in both Hennepin and
Ramsey Counties because of the provision in Minnesota law allowing

Table 4-3
Initial Registration Costs in the Twin Cities Area

Abstract continuation[a]	$ 45.00
Special assessments/tax search	15.00
District court fee	19.50
Publication costs[a]	50.00
Summons (one defendant)[a]	5.00
Certified copy (recorder)	3.50
Registration of decree	6.00
New certificate	8.00
Fund fee[a]	1.00
Legal fees	400.00 (to $600)
Total	$553.00 (to $750)

[a]Estimated minimum.

withdrawal only in counties without first-class cities. Thus, future landowners automatically acquire any benefits derived from registration. They also become obligated without choice to bear any burdens or costs that arise from the registered status of the land.

As a practical matter these costs are small compared to the expense of initial registration. They fall into three categories:

1. Costs in the form of official charges for the filing and entry of documents relating to subsequent transfers, adverse interests, and so on, which are higher than for unregistered land;
2. Costs in the form of official charges, as well as fees for attorneys when legal assistance might be needed, in those instances where special proceedings are required;
3. Costs borne by all taxpayers in the form of a subsidy required to operate and maintain the system.

The higher charges for registered land imposed by the office of the recorder/registrar are standard under the Minnesota law. The basic recording fee for nonregistered land is $1 per page, with a minimum of $3. In contrast, the fees for filings affecting registered land are fixed according to the kind of documentation or entry involved.

To illustrate the differences between the two fee structures, assume a routine transfer of a residence that involves (1) a deed conveying the property from the seller to the buyer; (2) the satisfaction of the seller's mortgage; and (3) the buyer's mortgage. Table 4-4 shows the differences in fees applicable to a transfer

Table 4-4
Minnesota Recording and Registration Fees

Torrens Fee	Description	Abstract Fee
N.C.	Filing of deed	$3.00
$ 8.00	Filing transfer; new certificate	N/A
3.50	Filing of mortgage satisfaction	3.00
N/A	Filing buyer's mortgage	3.00
3.50	Memorial fee, new mortgage	N/A
3.00	Mortgagee's duplicate	N/A
$18.00	*Total*	$9.00

of this kind. If the new mortgagee elects not to obtain a mortgagee's duplicate, the total Torrens fee in this typical transaction will be reduced $3, to $15, compared with $9 for unregistered property.

The differences between the two sets of charges reflect administrative obligations imposed by the requirements of the Torrens law. In both systems, certain legal documents must be filed to maintain their legal effectiveness. Torrens imposes the additional responsibilities of the retention and storage of the original documents and the meticulous preparation of certificates and the memorials to be entered thereon. Thus, the price differential between the two sets of charges for administering the respective programs appears to have a sound basis in the costs required to fulfill legal requirements.

In addition to the extra expense required to process routine transfers, the owner of registered land runs the risk that an additional set of costs might have to be accepted in the event of a contingency requiring the institution of special procedures. This risk is small. As discussed earlier, there was a total of 1,331 such proceedings held in 1976 in Hennepin County, an amount arising from approximately 105,000 parcels of registered land. Nevertheless, duplicate certificates are easily mislaid or lost, divorce is occurring with increasing frequency, and death under circumstances wherein the deceased's property must be transferred in accordance with a will or intestate distribution is not uncommon. Thus, the potential for the need to invoke special proceedings poses a realistic cost factor to any landowner.

The costs for such proceedings involve a registrar's filing fee, which ranges from $6.50 to replace a duplicate certificate on the basis of a court order to $42 to replace a duplicate based on the directive of the examiner, a court fee if a court proceeding is required, and the expense of legal assistance. Many such proceedings will in fact require the retention of an attorney. The proceeding before the examiner for the replacement of a lost duplicate could be handled by a landowner acting on his own, because of a lack of technical requirements. This is reported as not infrequent in Hennepin County but rare in Ramsey County.

In all other proceedings of this type, it appears that an attorney is almost indispensable. Conversations with local lawyers indicate that even the more routine of these proceedings require from one to two hours of professional time. Therefore, allowing $40 per hour as a fair billing rate for professional services, we estimate that the minimum cost to a landowner for legal fees would be in the range of $40 to $80 for many of these proceedings.

A final cost of the Minnesota Torrens system can be found in the form of a public subsidy. An excess of annual expenditures over revenues resulting from the Torrens operation creates a deficit, which is paid indirectly by all taxpayers in the respective counties and not just by registered landowners.

Under the Minnesota arrangement, the possible expenditures required to operate Torrens can be identified in four distinct operational units: the district court, the office of the chief examiner of titles, the office of the registrar of titles, and the office of the county treasurer for administration of the assurance fund. We disregard the last as insignificant from the standpoint of cost analysis.

We also disregard the expenditures involved in supporting the legal responsibilities of the courts. Because of the increasing role played by the examiner's office, the involvement of judges in providing direction to the operations in Hennepin and Ramsey Counties is minimal. It is possible, therefore, that the fees collected by the courts make their involvement financially self-sustaining on the basis of user-generated revenues alone.

In contrast, we find an imbalance of administrative expenditures in excess of income generated in the operation of both the chief examiner's and the registrar's offices. This is most obvious in the context of the operation of the examiner's office where no income at all is received. The 1977 budgets for the two offices in this area are as follows: Hennepin County, $183,600; Ramsey County, $78,000. The total budget for the Hennepin office is actually $229,500, but we have subtracted 20 percent of that amount as attributable to responsibilities unrelated to registered land.

The operations of the registrar's offices are also supported in part by the general taxpayers, but in a different way. Both of the offices we examined report annual data in a manner that makes it difficult to make meaningful comparisons between Torrens and the conventional recording system. Yet both operate at a substantial loss, presumably because of a combination of state and county policies calculated to achieve that result. Table 4-5 summarizes the financial experience of the two county offices.

These data reveal that Torrens revenues exceed those from conventional abstract recording despite the fact that there are fewer actual Torrens transactions. This is attributable to the higher fees assessed for Torrens activity because of the greater workload requirements imposed by the statute. Although

Table 4-5
Minnesota Registrar/Recorder Fiscal Summary (1976)

	Hennepin	Ramsey
Income:		
Torrens revenues	$263,906	$107,642
Abstract revenues	259,407	91,918
Other	56,509	4,631
Total	$579,822	$204,191
Expenditures:	865,187[a]	375,360
Net deficit	$285,365	$171,179

[a]Includes $47,137 in administrative overhead costs.

data on personnel allocations are not reported on a basis that facilitates easy comparison, we suspect that the increased revenues from Torrens filings roughly approximate the expenditures required. That is, the deficit resulting from the operation of the registrar/recorder's office is not one that favors Torrens over conventional recording. Instead, it appears to result from both systems, suggesting the applicability of a subsidy to each.

The fact that the Torrens system is, in fact, being subsidized in Minnesota raises policy questions beyond the purview of this study. What is important, we think, is the fact that the subsidy does exist. If the expense of Torrens administration were strictly allocated on a user basis, the true costs for initial registration and the subsequent administration of registered land would be higher than those currently sustained by registered landowners.

User Interests and Concerns

Reasons for Registration

In the Twin Cities area the prime reason for seeking land registration is the elimination of title defects. In addition, land registration provides some advantages in the form of standardization for complex commercial undertakings involving the parceling together of many different pieces of land.

Several factors are involved in the context of title-defect elimination. First, and perhaps historically the most significant, is the expeditious manner in which registration effects a quieting of title. If there is uncertainty or ambiguity in the history of a title, or a potential risk that threatens its marketability, the registration proceeding provides a simple and straightforward mechanism for the resolution of those problems. It has also proved to be a satisfactory method for clarifying the nature and extent of adverse claims and, although less frequently today, for the clarification of boundaries.

In this regard, the hallmark of registration is the legal finality that attaches to the initial registration decree. The effect of the decree is to kill off any historical or residual interests (other than those excepted by statute or case law) that may have denied the precision and clarity of title sought by land-owners and investors.

An alternative method for resolving title problems—such as that referred to in Minnesota as an action to determine adverse claims—is considered less desirable than registration. Lawyers feel that the decree resulting from such an action must be constantly reexamined for jurisdictional sufficiency, adequacy of notice to interested parties, and the like, and always has the potential for being qualified or limited at some unknown time in the future. In contrast, the registration decree is valid on its face, subject only to the few legal exceptions, and is immune from subsequent collateral attack.

Because of this legal conclusiveness, registration can play a risk-minimization role in situations where no perceived risk exists other than the remote possibility that a problem might occur, no matter how unlikely. Thus, in a commercial venture where the investment is substantial, the cost required for registration—in time as well as dollars—may be considered worthwhile for the conclusiveness and precision of title resulting from the registration decree.

Much the same reasoning is offered for situations in which several parcels of land have been pieced together. In such instances, there is always the possibility of a slight gap or overlap resulting from the packaging process. Registration eleminates this risk by unifying ownership within a single boundary description. In addition, it affords a framework for a greater simplicity for subsequent management of the packaged interests. It also provides a convenient method for clarifying interests vis-à-vis adjoining highways, in such cases as shopping centers, where entrance and exit considerations are of vital importance.

Significantly, reduction of transfer costs is not a reason for seeking land registration today. Historically, because of the custom in the area that sellers bear the cost of bringing the abstract up to date, developers of multi-parcel units found a distinct economic advantage under registration. The standardization of title for all units resulted in a cost for registered property abstracts that was considerably cheaper than conventional abstracts. The fact that the buyer and subsequent owners had to pay higher filing fees and other costs was of little consequence to the developer, who could easily compute the tradeoff between the expense of initial registration and the reduction of selling costs on the various units because of the cheaper abstracts.

Over the years, however, this incentive has been diminished because of technological improvements, such as the ready availability of cheap reproduction methods, which have narrowed the cost differential between the two kinds of abstracts. At today's costs, the approximately $20 to $25 saving that an RPA represents over a conventional residential abstract is not adequate to attract a developer to registration unless there are sufficient numbers of units involved to override the initial outlay for registration proceedings. That is, it would take at least forty units before the savings on registered abstracts would begin to equal minimum registration costs.

Persons Using Registration

The persons using land registration in the Twin Cities are predominantly landowners with defects in the title to the property. For the most part, the defects are of a kind that renders the land unsatisfactory for development or sale. Thus, the primary users of land registration are those who anticipate commerical gain from investing in real property. They include investors in office buildings, shopping centers, and industrial parks, and large multi-unit residential developers.

Earlier in the century, large undeveloped tracts—in the form of farms, timberland, and, in the Duluth area, mining properties—were placed into registration to protect against the loss of property from adverse possession and because of the economic incentive in the form of the fee structure for the assurance fund, which was computed on the basis of the unimproved value of the land only. However, land holdings of this kind are becoming increasingly rare because of growing urbanization.

For several decades, residential developers have been a major category of the users of the urban Minnesota Torrens systems. Although the incentive of reduced selling costs alluded to earlier has been substantially diminished, developers continue to use the Torrens system because of the acquisition of land that (1) had been registered earlier, for example, as farmland, or (2) had been the subject of tax forfeitures or foreclosure problems as the result of failures during the depression. Histories like the latter present a fairly typical situation in which Torrens principles serve to minimize identifiable title risks. The registration decree can put to rest any lingering doubts concerning the potential of an adverse or ambiguous history to affect current title status negatively.

Individual homeowners are not an identifiable class of users of Torrens except as purchasers of property that has already been registered. Stated another way, there is no identifiable incentive for a homeowner to seek registration except in instances where the need arises to clarify title status or boundaries. Since most homeowners find themselves in a situation where problems of this type have already been resolved (for example, as a result of the efforts of the developer or the original builder), the incidence of homeowner application for registration is not great. As a practical matter, there is no need for an individual to bear the costs of registration unless some circumstance exists that appears to justify the investment. This circumstance must be in the form of an identifiable threat or risk, since there is no distinct advantage to the status of land registration itself.

Impact on Closing Costs

One reason that land registration lacks a particular attraction for homeowners is the inability of the owner to treat registration expenses as a "pass through" improvement that could be recovered from a subsequent buyer. In theoretical terms, this means that registration status is not recognized as a distinctly measurable benefit that can function as an attribute of housing. In practical terms, it means that registration is not perceived by the various interests concerned with real estate as having any significant effect on closing costs at the time of subsequent resale.

We examined this aspect of Torrens impact from several points of view: from the perspective of lawyers who are real-estate specialists and who represent home buyers or sellers, developers, mortgage lenders, or others with interests in land; from the perspective of persons concerned with the administration of the Torrens systems; and from the perspective of thrift institutions and mortgage bankers, who have needs relating to title security that are independent of those of the homeowner. The reactions were virtually unanimous. While the Torrens system is highly respected and subsidized in the Twin Cities area, it fails to produce any significant reduction in the level of closing costs associated with the transfer of nonregistered residential property.

Earlier in this chapter we noted that registered property abstracts for residential property tend to run $20 to $25 cheaper, on the average, than conventional abstracts. Because of the custom in Minnesota that home sellers bear the cost of abstract continuation, this translates to a net saving for the seller. We also noted an increase in public recording fees (to the buyer) of $9. The effect, of course, is a net saving of $11 to $16 in favor of the transaction involving registered property.

More important, perhaps, are the expenses generated for the services rendered in relation to determining title status and validity. Consistent with the established patterns in the Twin Cities area, these services are largely rendered by private attorneys. Further, the expenses for legal services of this kind manifest themselves in two respects: first, in costs sustained by mortgage lenders, which are passed directly on to the buyer/borrower at closing; and second, in the fees of attorneys engaged by buyers to represent their independent interests in the transaction.

As to the expenses encountered by lenders, we found that there was, as a general rule, no distinction attributable to either the presence or absence of registered land. Typically, the fees charged by lawyers were based on either a flat rate (for example, $35 to $40 for each abstract examined) or a step rate predicated on the amount of the loan (for example, $35 up to $30,000 plus $1 for each $1,000 thereafter). These charges are for the examination of an abstract (RPA or conventional) that has been brought current at the seller's expense. They do not include services that might be required to resolve problems discovered in the examination of the abstract. Nor do they include additional effort that might be required for particularly difficult title histories, which are not common in residential property but are less likely to occur with Torrens land.

In addition, our conversations with mortgage lenders revealed that registered land contributed to neither an advantage nor a disadvantage in terms of processing costs. Thus, origination fees or other flat charges imposed by lenders are the same without regard to the legal status of the property to be subjected to a purchase mortgage interest. Further, as discussed in the following section, the motivations that convince lenders of the need to require title insurance exist independently of, and therefore are unrelated to, Torrens principles. That is, in the Twin Cities area, title insurance is frequently obtained for both registered and unregistered property.

Most of the considerations discussed here apply with equal force to the expenses encountered by a buyer who engages an attorney to represent his or her interests in a residential transaction. One of the responsibilities of the attorney would be to examine the abstract—usually the same one examined by the lender's attorney—and issue an opinion as to title. This, of course, is the same function exercised by the lender's attorney. We found, however, that the law firms representing large institutional lenders had the benefit of specialization and streamlined procedures, which generally did not apply to attorneys representing home buyers. The fee customarily charged for title examination by buyer's attorneys runs higher than that charged by lender's attorneys, for example, $60 compared with $45 for an average residence.

We interviewed one lawyer who indicated a capability to reduce that part of his customary fee related to title examination by as much as 25 percent, $15 of $60, because of the amount of time saved in examining an RPA. Others agreed that RPAs did present some time saving in examination. But where typical residential property is involved, it was indicated that any saving was in minutes only, not enough to justify a fee reduction. The consensus was to the effect that customary legal fees for examining title to household property do not vary in the Twin Cities area because of the existence of registered land.

Moreover, it appears that the going rate for home-buyer representation is in the general neighborhood of $200, of which only about $50 to $75 is attributable to services related to title examination. In other words, lawyers in the area estimate that, on the average, representation of a home buyer requires four to five hours of involvement, of which only one hour or less is devoted to title examination. The balance is taken up by client interviews, examination and/or negotiation of the purchase agreement, handling of details in the interim between contract and closing, and representation at the closing.

Relationship to Title Insurance

A final consideration relevant to closing costs is the extent to which land registration affects either the need for title insurance or, given a continued need, the rates at which it is available. In both instances, we found the effect to be negligible. The registered status of a land parcel does not ameliorate or otherwise alter the circumstances leading to a decision to seek title insurance. And there is no differential between the charges assessed for insuring registered land as opposed to unregistered land.

For residential property, a major factor relevant to title insurance is the policy of the primary mortgage lending institution. Lenders who are prime sources of homeowner mortgage money in the Twin Cities area (for example, thrift institutions and mortgage bankers) are motivated by many of the same considerations that affect the behavior of their counterparts in other parts of the country. Specifically: (1) In new construction (that is, residential property under development), title insurance is required in virtually all instances, because of the potential for adverse mechanic's liens. Since mechanic's liens are one of the key types of claims valid against registered land without being recorded and memorialized on the certificate, Torrens principles do not work to prevent claims from arising that would be senior to the security interest of the mortgagee. (2) Where the homeowner's mortgage is to be insured by one of the federal insurance programs (FHA or VA), title insurance is a standard requirement imposed by all lending sources. Registered land does not alter this requirement. (3) If it is contemplated that a mortgage will or might have to be sold into the secondary market, title insurance is required in order to facilitate the sale in response to the terms of institutional investors. Again the requirement is imposed independent of the registered status of the property subject to the mortgage. Currently, this is probably the strongest motivation shaping the attitude of lenders with respect to their title insurance needs.

There is some variance in the ways in which Twin City mortgage lenders implement these policies with respect to title-insurance requirements. The approaches described for new construction and federally insured mortgages seem to be common to all lenders; thus, it is predictable that title insurance will be required on all mortgages without regard to the registered status of the property.

When secondary market considerations arise, however, the requirements established by lenders are directly dependent on the degree to which they sell mortgages into the secondary market. For example, mortgage bankers and some thrift institutions in the Twin Cities area view themselves as mortgage originators only. Because of individual business and financial perspectives, lenders of this type plan to sell all of their mortgage holdings. Accordingly, title insurance is a fixed requirement for all properties involved.

Other thrift institutions, particularly the larger ones in the area, view the secondary market as a contingency factor related to liquidity management and attempt to maintain internal management policies assuring that some part of their portfolio will be suitable for resale, if needed. The institutions pursuing these objectives require title insurance only on those mortgages expected to fulfill the prescribed portfolio balance. This is sometimes achieved by random selection. Again, the existence of registered status is not considered an element in the selection criteria. Where title insurance is considered necessary, it will be required for both registered and residential property.

General Observations

It is clear from our observations that the Torrens system in Hennepin and Ramsey Counties has worked well, and continues to work well, in fulfilling the needs of landowners, investors, and others for an expeditious legal mechanism to clarify and/or remove questions of title arising from uncertain histories. However, while the objectives of title simplification and minimization of historical defects must be considered as being substantially fulfilled, it is clear that land registration has not provided positive impact in the direction of reducing title-related closing costs for the average home buyer and seller.

For the most part, we attribute the successes of the Torrens system in this area to the professional caliber and devotion of the various judges, examiners, and registrars who have held these positions over the years. It is clear from the persons we interviewed that the system as a whole, and its various administrative components, holds the confidence and respect of the wide range of interests concerned with local real property. This apparently is not true of the Torrens systems administered in other parts of the seven-county metropolitan area or in many other counties in the state. While we did not have occasion to observe these other Torrens systems, we heard substantial criticism, in some cases harsh, from lawyers and others who had a framework of experience from which comparisons could be made. We assume that the difference is attributable to the superior quality and constructiveness of the professionalism that past and current administrators have brought to bear in developing and shaping the respective programs in the Twin Cities area.

5

Massachusetts

Introduction and Background

Introduction

The statutory provisions for the registration of land in Massachusetts were first enacted in 1898. The current statute consists of approximately 120 sections, comprising Chapter 185 of the Massachusetts General Laws (MGL). Despite frequent amendments over the years, much of the original act remains intact, especially those parts that provide the basic principles underlying the operation of the registration system.

In all important respects, the Massachusetts approach to land registration adheres closely to the basic Torrens principles. However, it is unique among the systems we have observed and studied in several respects: first, Massachusetts has a centralized statewide system, with all initial registrations processed and decrees issued by a single judicial/administrative unit; second, it is administered by a court—originally created as the court of registration, but now known as the land court—consisting of one judge and two associate judges whose jurisdiction is limited to land registration and other matters confined to real estate; and third, it requires that boundaries be registered along with title, with the result that all property descriptions are tied to common and permanent monuments.

These attributes of the Massachusetts system have made it the subject of considerable intellectual curiosity and some duplication. It is reported, for example, that the Massachusetts statute was copied verbatim early in the century for application to the Hawaii territory and the Philippine Islands. In addition, the chief engineer of the land court—who bears the administrative responsibility for surveying and boundary determination—reports that the engineering aspects of the Massachusetts system have been closely studied by representatives of many foreign nations.

We attempted to concentrate our observations on the impact of land registration in Suffolk County. Suffolk County includes the cities of Chelsea, Revere, and Winthrop, along with Boston, and forms the core of the principal urban area in the state. It is also the major business location of the land court. As a result, Suffolk County has a substantial history of experience with land registration. It is estimated that approximately 20 percent of the land parcels in the county are registered.

Virtually all important characteristics of the Massachusetts system apply uniformly throughout the state. This is because of the statewide jurisdiction of the land court. However, the use patterns vary greatly. In the sparsely settled semimountainous western counties, land registration has been rarely used. In contrast, parts of the southeastern coastal area, including Plymouth and Barnstable (Cape Cod) Counties and the neighboring islands of Martha's Vineyard and Nantucket, have been the subject of registration activity that exceeds that of Suffolk County. For example, we were quoted estimates that as much as three quarters of Nantucket Island is currently registered. If this is accurate, then Nantucket County has the highest percentage of registered land in the United States.

Local Real-Estate Customs and Practices

In the Boston area— indeed, in much of New England—the predominant method used for title assurance is search-and-examination efforts of private attorneys. While private abstracting companies exist, it is common for attorneys to search the title themselves or have it searched under their supervision. Thus, the notion of bringing an existing abstract up to date for a particular sale transaction is not the standardized procedure we found in Minnesota. Massachusetts does not have a marketable title act as such. Therefore, lawyers in the Suffolk County area typically search a title back for sixty years or more.

Subsequent to the search, the lawyer examines the title history and certifies its status in a letter to the client, which will indicate any existing encumbrances and, where appropriate, the lawyer's interpretation of the significance of those encumbrances. The lawyer's opinion is backed up by professional (malpractice) liability insurance. However, liability under Massachusetts law lies only in the case of negligence. Further, the lawyer's certification is valid as against record defects only. Possible deficiencies or encumbrances arising from circumstances not reflected in the public records are not covered by the lawyer's certification.

The custom in the Suffolk County area is that the buyer in a typical residential sale bears all title-related costs (except for preparation of the seller's deed and for efforts that may be required to clear any defects revealed by the search and examination of title). This expense arises in two ways: in costs incurred by the mortgage lender and passed through to the buyer at closing; and in costs incurred directly by the buyer through personal legal representation.

There is substantial variance in the Suffolk County area in the approach by mortgage lenders to the retention of attorneys for title-related work. Some use only a single law firm. Others provide a prospective borrower with a list of approved attorneys and allow the borrower/home buyer to shop around and choose the attorney who will do the work. Unlike many states, Massachusetts has a conveyancer's bar association that is separate and distinct from the general bar association. This helps to facilitate the custom of allowing the borrower to select an attorney from an extensive list provided by the lender.

Even with borrower selection (and ultimate payment of the expense), it is clear that the lawyer chosen is principally obligated to serve the lender, not the borrower. In fact, Massachusetts has a statute that requires that borrowers be provided with a written notice to this effect in conjunction with the mortgage application. The result is that buyers frequently retain their own additional lawyer. As we found in the other jurisdictions, the impression of those who regularly work in the real-estate area is that the incidence of home-buyer legal representation has been increasing over the last few years, probably because of the dramatic increase in the cost of residential property. Whatever the reason, a part of the service an attorney will render for a home-buyer client is the search and examination of the title to the property in question.

Title insurance for residential property is not commonly used in the Boston/ Suffolk County area. One reason cited to us is a long-standing tradition of accuracy and reliability in the recording systems. Another is that, traditionally, the major mortgage lenders in the area—principally mutual savings banks—have not been sellers on the secondary mortgage market. To the contrary, Boston-area thrift institutions have generally played an important role as buyers of mortgages generated in other areas. To some extent, this has changed with the repeating cycles of disintermediation in the last decade. However, a pattern still remains. Although we found some evidence to suggest a growing usage, title insurance in the Boston area is still associated more with commercial than residential property. As a result, title companies do not maintain their own title plants, and insurance is issued on the basis of the certification of title by private attorneys.

The Torrens Operation

The Land Court

The land court was originally created in order to provide a firm constitutional basis for the registration procedure and an administrative framework for the development and continuation of the expertise required to deal with the intricacies of real-property law.

Originally, it was established as an inferior court; all orders and decrees were subject to appeal to the superior court, the basic court of general law and equity jurisdiction. Through successive amendments, the status of the land court was gradually elevated to that of a court of record on a par with the superior court—with which it shares concurrent jurisdiction today on a great many real-estate matters. The three judges who comprise the court are appointed for life terms.

Currently, the land court has, in addition to exclusive jurisdiction over land registration and related matters affecting registered land, original jurisdiction over a wide variety of cases affecting unregistered land. As a practical matter, however, the bulk of the judicial activities of the court—estimated by the chief judge to be in the range of 60 to 70 percent—arises from the registration system.

The chief administrative official of the land court is the recorder, an office that corresponds in function to that called the clerk in most other courts. The total staff consists of sixty-five persons, including the three judges. Approximately one-third of the staff, or twenty-one persons, are employed by the engineering section, which is administered by the engineer for the court. The balance of the staff is concerned with legal/processing functions and includes ten attorneys, one of whom bears the title of chief title examiner.

The land court has only indirect supervision over the day-to-day maintenance of the registration system after the issuance of initial registration decrees. This responsibility is entrusted to the register of deeds in each county, which is an elected position. Under the Massachusetts statute, the register is automatically an assistant recorder[a] of the land court. In addition, the three most populous counties have staff authorization for a technical assistant whose duties are devoted full-time to the administration of registered land. However, the salaries of the officials and staff in the register/assistant recorder's office are under the budgetary controls of the respective county governments, separate and distinct from those applicable to the land court itself.

General Description

A landowner seeking registration in Massachusetts applies to the land court for a judicial decree. The application must be accompanied by a comprehensive survey of the land in question. The registration proceeding involves a thorough review of the survey as well as of the status of legal title. The registration decree is accompanied by, and referenced to, an official plan of the property. The net effect is a declaration of ownership that is certain and indefeasible as to boundaries as well as title.

Subsequent to registration, a certified copy of the decree, together with a copy of the decree plan, is forwarded to the Registry of Deeds for the county in which the property is located. As indicated earlier each elected register of deeds automatically holds the position of assistant recorder for that county. After receipt of the registration decree and related papers, the local assistant recorder prepares an original certificate of title, which remains on file, and a duplicate certificate, which is delivered to the owner (see page 24).

---

[a]This nomenclature is almost directly opposite to that used in other jurisdictions. In Minnesota and Illinois, the term *recorder* refers to the official administering the conventional deed-recording system and *registrar* refers to the official administering registered titles.

Subsequent transfers of the property are accomplished by the filing with the local assistant recorder of a deed from the registered owner, together with the owner's duplicate. The existing certificate of title is then cancelled, and a new certificate is prepared in the name of the new owner, along with a new owner's duplicate. Adverse interests affecting the land are also filed with the local assistant recorder, whereupon memoranda are then entered on the appropriate certificate of title. Proceedings must be initiated in the land court in order to obtain a replacement of an owner's duplicate, to effect a change in ownership without the voluntary consent of the registered owner, or to make any other change to the status of title as described by the certificate.

As a result of the registration decree and the subsequent registration process, a good-faith purchaser takes title free and clear of any and all encumbrances, interests, or claims that are not reflected or memorialized on the face of the certificate. This general rule is subject to certain statutory exceptions noted in the following section. Interests in registered land cannot be obtained by adverse possession, prescription, or other implication based on possession or usage.

As a general rule, land cannot be withdrawn from registration once the initial registration decree is issued. The statute contemplates that the registered status shall continue in perpetuity. The only practical exception arises in the context of condominiums intended to be built on land that is only partially registered.

The land court also administers a land title "confirmation" process in addition to the registration system. Under confirmation, the court issues a decree confirming title in the petitioner's name, subject to valid encumbrances as of the date of decree. Boundaries are not confirmed, however, and the land is not subjected to the subsequent certification procedures used for registered land. That is, subsequent transfers are administered through the conventional deed-recording system.

Exceptions

Similar to Torrens legislation in other states, the Massachusetts Land Registration Act provides certain statutory exceptions to the general rule that purchasers of registered land hold that property free of all encumbrances except those noted on the certificate of title. These are set forth in Section 46, Chapter 185, MGL.

1. Liens, claims, or rights in land arising from the Constitution or the laws of the United States or from Massachusetts statutes, which are not required to be recorded in the registry of deeds to be legally valid against unregistered lands;

2. Taxes within two years after they have been committed to the office legally designated for collection;
3. Highways, town ways, and any private way laid out by statutory procedure if the certificate does not state that the boundaries thereto have been determined;
4. Leases for terms not exceeding seven years;
5. Liability from assessments for betterments and other statutory liability, other than for taxes, which attaches to land as a lien;
6. Liens in favor of the United States for unpaid taxes pursuant to the Internal Revenue Code of 1954, as amended.

Unlike other jurisdictions, the Massachusetts courts have not carved out any additional exceptions to the legal conclusiveness of the certificate of title. Thus, the purchaser of registered land needs to be concerned only with the possibility of an interest, claim, or right arising from the statutory exceptions.

As a practical matter, this means that the attorney representing a prospective purchaser must inquire into local taxes and assessments, federal tax claims or liens, possible bankruptcy proceedings, and the existence of parties in possession under short-term leases. The exception for public highways, town ways, and private rights, if any, is not of great practical significance because of the land court's policy to examine and register all boundaries.

One exception, which is of much current interest, arises from litigation concerning the claims of Indian tribes to substantial land holdings. The claim of the Wampanoag tribe to the town of Mashpee in Barnstable County (Cape Cod) is illustrative. Since the claim is based on federal law, the registered status of parcels of land in Mashpee may offer no greater legal protection than that available to nonregistered land. The matter has not been resolved but is the subject of much discussion because of the pendency of the Wampanoag claim.

Mechanics of Registration

Registration in Massachusetts is initiated by petition to the land court. The petition recites the petitioner's claim of title to the land (by reference to a recorded deed or to probate proceedings), any appurtenant right (for example, easement or right-of-way across adjoining land) sought to be registered, the assessed value of the land and buildings as of the date of filing, any outstanding mortgages, and names and addresses of adjoining property owners, together with other information peculiar to the land in question. The petition must be accompanied by a surveyor's plan and a certification of adjoining owners by the appropriate municipal assessor. Simultaneous with the filing of the petition for registration, a notice of the filing is filed with the registry of deeds for the county in which the land is located.

The survey plan presented by the petitioner must be prepared and certified by a registered land surveyor in accordance with a manual of instructions published by the engineering department of the land court. The plan must also conform to the requirements of local planning boards and, in some cases, must be approved by the local board.

At the time of filing, the petitioner pays a minimum fee of $150. This amount is treated as a deposit against the petitioner's account. Since the number of potential legal defendants varies from case to case, the cost of legal notice and publication may require that additional sums be advanced. In addition to the land court fee of $150, the petitioner must also pay the amount equal to one-tenth of one percent ($1 per $1,000) of the assessed value of the property. This amount, in turn, is paid into the assurance fund maintained by the state treasurer.

After filing, one of the judges of the land court refers the title for examination to one of the approved examiners of title who has been appointed as such pursuant to Section 12 of Chapter 185. This examiner is required to be a qualified attorney but is not the staff member of the court who bears the title of chief title examiner or title examiner. In practice, the suggestion by the attorney representing the petitioner of an examiner appointed under Section 12 will be honored by the court. The examiner must be disinterested and cannot be the attorney representing the petitioner. However, the fee for the examiner's services is payable by the petitioner directly.

The appointed examiner prepares an abstract of the title to the property and performs a thorough examination. It is expected that the search will go back at least fifty to sixty years and will include all relevant records. The report of the examiner to the court includes the abstract and amounts in practical effect to a presentation of title. It identifies potential defendants as to the petitioner's claim to the property.

Once the examiner's report is filed, it is processed for service of notice and publication. As a matter of course, landowners adjoining the property will be served with notice of the proceeding by registered mail, as well as all potential defendants identified in the examiner's report. In addition, the statute requires publication in a newspaper of general circulation in the county in which the property is located and the posting of notice on the property. The citations and publication are prepared by the land court staff.

If the case is uncontested, the file is forwarded to the judge for examination. Under the land court staffing pattern, each judge has a full-time title examiner who is an attorney admitted to legal practice. The title examiner studies the abstract and report of the independent examiner, verifies the adequacy of notice and publication, reviews the surveyor's plan, and identifies any evidentiary requirements necessary to support the petition for registration.

After all evidentiary requirements have been met, an order for decree is prepared and the file is forwarded to the engineering department of the court.

The responsibility of this department is to prepare an official plan in accordance with the dictates of the order for decree. This involves the review of the initial plan prepared by the petitioner's surveyor and a reconciliation of the property in question with adjoining registered land, streets, and highways. Although permanent monuments (stone bounds) will have been established pursuant to the original survey, the engineering department may insist on the erection of additional monuments.

After preparation of the official (decree) plan of the property, a final decree is prepared and signed by the judge. At this point, notice is provided interested parties who may have reserved the right to inspect the final plan before it is issued. This might occur in the case of an adjoining landowner who did not wish to contest the petitioner's claim to title but was concerned over the accuracy of the boundary lines established by the decree plan prepared by the engineering department.

Once the registration decree is entered, the essential papers (for example, copy of decree, the decree plan, original of mortgage if any) are forwarded to the assistant recorder (register of deeds) for the appropriate county. At the registry, the title is run down since the date of the original notice of filing. If no change has occurred, the decree is entered and an appropriate certificate of title (along with an owner's duplicate certificate) is prepared. If some change affecting the status of title has occurred, the matter will be referred back to the land court for appropriate disposition.

Mechanics after Registration; Subsequent Legal Proceedings

After title and boundaries are registered by decree of the land court, all documents affecting title must be filed with the registered-land section of the Registry of Deeds for the county or district in which the land is located. Under Massachusetts law, documents reflecting claims and interests retain their legal effectiveness against the owner in his or her personal capacity whether or not filed. However, the claims and interests do not legally attach to the land unless the documents are filed and memorialized on the certificate of title. Thus, except for the statutory exceptions described earlier, a good-faith purchaser is entitled to the property free and clear of any interest or encumbrance not noted on the certificate. Or, in the words of Section 54 of the legislation, the official certificate of title in the registration book maintained by the assistant recorder (or a duly certified copy) "shall be received as evidence in all courts of the Commonwealth, and shall be conclusive as to all matters contained therein . . . ."

Under the Massachusetts approach to Torrens, except for wills and leases under seven years, documents executed by an owner with respect to registered land serve as evidence of authority to the assistant recorder to register the conveyance or to take other action that affects the land. If the document is voluntarily executed by the owner, as in the case of a deed or mortgage, the owner's duplicate certificate must be presented along with the instrument before a new certificate can be prepared and entered or a memorandum be made upon an existing certificate. The presentation of the duplicate is "conclusive authority" to the recorder and is legally binding upon all persons claiming under the registered owner. Without the presentation of the duplicate, as a general rule the recorder has no authorization to act except by order of the land court.

Special provisions exist in the statute for the assistant recorder to act in cases where the land is registered in the name of a trust or has become the subject of a trust (Sections 72 to 76), in cases involving insolvency or bankruptcy (Section 94), and in cases involving the death of the registered owner (Section 97). In such instances, the act of entering a new certificate or preparing a memorandum on the existing certificate is premised on legal authority specifically set forth in a voluntary instrument executed by the registered owner (for example, a trust instrument), in a court decree (for example, in bankruptcy or in probate), or in another legal document (for example, a death certificate attesting to the death of a joint owner). The instrument, document, or decree is filed with and retained by the assistant recorder. If there is any doubt as to the interpretation to be given an instrument or the proper memorandum to be entered on a certificate, the matter can be resolved only by the land court.

Similar provisions exist with respect to actions of the assistant recorder with respect to claims and interests adverse to the registered owner. Attachments, liens, judgments, and other claims and interests arising from other than the voluntary act of the owner are filed with the local assistant recorder and entered by memorandum on the certificate. However, the assistant recorder's statutory discretion is limited to the ascertainment of the proper legal form of the instruments offered for filing. Neither the act of filing nor the entry of a memorandum on the certificate has the legal effect of qualifying or resolving an adverse claim. Further, the local assistant recorder lacks the authority to correct an error in a certificate, or a memorandum recorded thereon, or to remove a memorandum that is obsolete or otherwise legally ineffective.

In all instances where the local assistant recorder lacks the authority to act, a party seeking a change in ownership status from that represented by the certificate of title must petition the land court for appropriate relief. Known as subsequent, or "S," proceedings, one of the most common involves seeking authorization for the replacement of a lost owner's duplicate certificate. Other examples include:

1. Certain circumstances involving the death of the registered owner (that is, where the decedent is the last survivor of previously deceased joint owners or where a sale of land is to take place pursuant to a power of sale in a will or a license to sell granted in probate);

2. Instances (such as in divorce) where ownership has legally vested in a party other than the owner reflected on the certificate but the owner's duplicate cannot be presented or is not available to accomplish the transfer;
3. Where interests reflected on the certificate require amendment, alteration, or deletion because of error in transcription, the failure of a contingency or other condition giving rise to a legal termination, a change of name of a registered owner (whether by marriage or otherwise), dissolution of a corporate owner, and the like;
4. A "tax taking" by a city or town seeking the land for nonpayment of taxes; and
5. A petition to eliminate or alter a way, reverse the flow of a brook, or otherwise alter the official surveying plan.

Because of the statewide jurisdiction of the land court, "S" proceedings provide a substantial share of the court's registered land activity. In the fiscal year ending June 30, 1975, the court handled more than 1,500 cases of this type, a level of activity consistent with its work load in prior years. The filing fee for proceedings of this type is small, only $5. As a practical matter, the overwhelming majority are routine, uncontested matters, which are handled informally, without the need for a full hearing.

A major function of the land court's chief title examiner is to examine the papers offered in these proceedings and advise the judges of the propriety of the relief sought. However, despite their informality and appropriateness for summary treatment, "S" proceedings inevitably involve the assistance of an attorney. We are advised that it is infrequent for a landowner to appear in his own behalf, even in a proceeding to replace a lost duplicate certificate. In this connection, it should be noted that the offices of the land court are located in Boston—meaning that a landowner or other party interested in registered land in other parts of the state must either retain an attorney in the Boston area or incur the time and costs for travel.

The Assurance Fund

Consistent with the statewide operation of the Massachusetts land registration program, there is a single statewide assurance fund. This fund was created for the purpose of compensating for losses arising from the administration of registered land after initial registration. Unlike other American Torrens systems, there is no provision for compensation for losses sustained as a result of the initial registration decree.

Fund Administration

The fund is generated by the assessment of a fee at the time of initial registration in the amount of one-tenth of one percent ($1 per $1,000) of the most recent assessment of the property for municipal taxation. Under Massachusetts law, property should be assessed at fair market value. However, there is much recent litigation (unrelated to registered land) contesting the fact that this has not been the practice.

The fees collected by the recorder of the land court are paid to the state treasurer, who maintains the assurance fund under the law. There is, however, no provision in the law for distinguishing between the assets of the fund and other assets of the Commonwealth.

Section 104 of Chapter 185, MGL, provides that, if the fund is deficient (apparently for any reason—the law does not specify), the treasurer shall make up the deficiency from any state funds not otherwise appropriated. However, subsequent sums received for the fund must be repaid first to the general treasury until the amount paid for the deficiency is recovered. This implies that current accounts of the Commonwealth back up the assurance fund to the extent that unappropriated funds exist, but that the general assets of the Commonwealth are not otherwise available.

As of January 1, 1977, the assurance fund consisted in a value of $346,000. In our opinion this is relatively small considering the fact that it applies statewide. However, our interviews with interested parties did not reveal any particular concern about the size of the fund.

Claims Management

Over the years very few claims have been brought against the Massachusetts fund. Professor Powell's 1938 study reported that the total of payments from the fund to that time amounted only $2,300, and that these had occurred years earlier. Since that time, some claims have been brought and paid from the fund. Although the data are unclear as to precisely how many and in what amounts, the consensus is that claims have been relatively rare. Moreover, it is clear from the annual reports of the state treasurer that no amounts have been paid from the fund in the last ten years. The most recent reported appellate decision pertaining to a claim against the fund is dated 1962.

As indicated earlier, the approach of Massachusetts to the compensatory purpose of the fund is unique in that it is intended for losses sustained subsequent to initial registration. Section 101 of Chapter 185, MGL, provides that:

A person, who, without negligence on his part, sustains loss or damage, or is deprived of land or of any estate or interest therein *after the initial registration of land*, by the negotiation of another person as owner of such land, or of any interest therein, through fraud or in consequence of any error, omission, mistake or misdescription in any certificate of title or in any entry or memorandum in the registration book, may recover in contract in the superior court compensation for such loss or damage or for such land or estate or interest therein from the assurance fund. (*Emphasis supplied.*)

This seems to impose a hardship on persons who might have an interest improperly cut off at the time of initial registration. The only protections for such persons are the procedural protections in the statute and the extreme care taken by the land court in examining applications.

Section 101 also provides that a potential claimant against the fund must exhaust all other legal remedies as a condition precedent to recovery. No appellate decisions are available to interpret the full meaning of this provision. It seems, however, to encourage litigation and/or to discourage the private settlement of claims.

Further, it is not clear whether the loss or damage that the fund is intended to compensate includes expenses for legal and related representation necessary to prosecute the claim. The language just quoted seems to imply the contrary. Again, there is a lack of appellate decisions to clarify the point.

Economic Considerations

Frequency and Extent of Registration

Since 1898 the land court has issued more than 30,000 decrees registering title to one or more parcels of land. Because of the split in administration—with the statewide land court issuing initial decrees but local assistant recorders preparing individual title certificates—there is no reliable method to estimate the exact number of registered land units in the state today. Because of the fact that one registered tract can, upon subdivision, give rise to several registered parcels, and because there is a high degree of coincidence between registration and residential development we received estimates quantifying land registration for the entire state that ranged from a low of 100,000 to a high of 350,000 land parcels.

At the level of the individual county, however, more reliable estimates are available because of a statutory requirement that assistant recorders number certificates in consecutive order. As of the close of business on December 31, 1976, the most recent certificate entered in Suffolk County was numbered 88,507. Allowing for replications—because a certificate prepared for a new owner will involve a separate number for the same land parcel and because subsequent subdivision will result in one more numbered certificate than the actual number of subdivided units—we estimate that there are approximately 20,000 registered land parcels in the county. This amounts to 19 percent of the approximately 105,000 parcels in the county, an estimate obtained from the assessing offices of the four cities that make up Suffolk County.

This is a rough equivalent of the percentage reached by comparing the annual number of certificates entered for registered land with deeds recorded for unregistered land. The figures set forth in table 5-1 show a fairly steady percentage of registered-land activity, in the neighborhood of 16 to 17 percent for Suffolk County.

Conversations with interested parties in the Boston area reveal that the incidence of land registration in Suffolk County has dropped off considerably in the last twenty to thirty years. Early in the century, land in the city of Boston enjoyed the lion's share of the land court's attention. After World War II, the spread of the urban population away from the city led to an increasing amount of registration in the three suburban counties surrounding Suffolk—Essex, Norfolk, and Middlesex Counties. More recently, the trend has been in the direction of the southeastern coastal areas of the state—Plymouth, Barnstable, Dukes, and Nantucket Counties—although land in each of these counties was the subject of a considerable amount of registration as much as fifty years ago.

During this transition between different areas in the state, the frequency of new registrations has declined somewhat. Data from the land court reveal a fairly constant average of initial registration decrees, in the neighborhood of 400 per annum over the last decade. (Data for the last six years are provided in table 5-2.) This is substantially below the peak year of 1957, when the court issued 910 registration decrees. However, it is fairly consistent with the underlying forces that lead landowners to seek registration. As population growth subsides, along with residential development, it is probable that initial registrations in Massachusetts will gradually decline and that the amount of the land court's time devoted to the supervision of already registered land will steadily increase.

Table 5-1
Real-Estate Transactions in Suffolk County

	Certificates Issued: Registered Land	Deeds Filed: Nonregistered Land
1976	1,124	6,213
1975	1,053	5,257
1974	1,128	5,495
1973	1,462	6,899

Table 5-2
Massachusetts Land Court Registration
Decrees

Fiscal Year	Registration Decrees
1970-1971	413
1971-1972	356
1972-1973	359
1973-1974	445
1974-1975	390
1975-1976	485

Cost of Initial Registration

The cost of initial registration in Massachusetts is the highest of the three systems we had the opportunity to examine. This is attributable to two distinct
features of the Massachusetts approach to land registration: first, the requirement that boundaries be registered—which manifests itself in the form of a
surveyor's fee for the landowner/petitioner, together with the higher official
fee for the registration process; and second, in the form of the fee for the
services of the private attorney/examiner.

The effect of these requirements is to impose three distinct but variable
fees for professional services on the landowner/petitioner seeking registration:
for legal representation; for surveying; and for the attorney/examiner appointed
by the court. These expenditures are in addition to the minimum court fee
of $150, plus one-tenth of one percent of the assessed value of the land for
the assurance fund, and are not reflected in the public records maintained by
the court. Our interviews with attorneys, surveyors, and officials of the land
court provided the basis for the estimates in table 5-3 for the prevailing charges
in the area. For the purposes of the contribution to the assurance fund, we
assume an assessed value of the property at $50,000.

The total expense is substantial. In our opinion, however, based on our
interviews, it is not inconsistent with the services being rendered. Moreover,
the expenditures involved are based on the time required to provide the services, rather than the value of the property. Thus, the costs remain relatively
constant, independent of the amount or value of the land. The major variables
arise from the degree of difficulty that might be encountered in a particular
instance. For example, it was suggested to us that the high prevalence of
marshland in parts of Plymouth and Barnstable Counties imposes barriers
to access that frequently raise the cost of surveying to more than $1,000.

Table 5-3
Initial Registration Costs in Massachusetts

Land court fee	$ 150
Assurance fund contribution (est.)	50
Attorney's fee	400 (to $600)
Surveyor's fee	500 (to $700)
Examiner's fee	400 (to $600)
	$1,500 (to $2,100)

From the standpoint of time, the initial registration process requires anywhere from a year to eighteen months. A lot depends on the extent to which the petitioner encourages the appointed examiner to move diligently toward the filing of his report. The impression we have from conversations with officials of the land court is that it is rare to complete a registration in less than one year and that the average period of time required is in the neighborhood of fifteen to eighteen months. If the application is contested, both the time and expense required are likely to increase.

Cost of Subsequent Activity

After initial registration, the registered landowner in Massachusetts continues to pay for the registered status in the form of public charges for the registration of subsequent transfers, mortgages, and the like, which are slightly higher than those for the filing and recording of documents for nonregistered land. In addition, there is a built-in cost in the form of the potential risk of needing legal assistance for subsequent proceedings in the land court, for example, to replace a lost owner's duplicate.

The differential in public charges for the filing and recording of transfers and other documents reflecting interests in land is represented in table 5-4. In a typical sale of residential property—involving a deed, the satisfaction of the seller's mortgage, and entry of the buyer's mortgage—the recorder fees for registered land will amount to $38, compared with a total of $25 in registry fees for nonregistered land. As in the other Torrens jurisdictions, the higher charges are attributable to the extra effort required to process documents pertaining to registered land—that is, the preparation of new certificates and the entry of memoranda on certificates—and the higher degree of professional skill involved in interpreting the legal significance of documents, preventing errors, and the like.

In the event of a situation requiring the institution of subsequent

Table 5-4
Suffolk County Recording and Registration Fees

	Registered Land	Nonregistered Land
Deed (incl. new certificate	$15	$10
Mortgage	15	10
All other documents	8	5

proceedings, the basic cost to the landowner will involve expenditures for legal assistance, a $5 land court fee, and, if required the few dollars involved for certified copies of public documents, for example, a death certificate or a divorce decree. Since most proceedings of this type are fairly routine, we estimate that the demand on an attorney's time will average between two and four hours. Thus, at a basic compensation rate of $40 per hour, the anticipated minimum expense to a registered landowner will be in the range of $80 to $160. Of course, situations requiring subsequent proceedings do not necessarily arise for every landowner. However, they can arise from common human circumstances, such as death, divorce, or the misplacement of the owner's duplicate certificate. Thus, the costs involved fall in the category of a potential expense that every registered landowner must bear.

Cost of Administration

The operation of the land court in Massachusetts is substantially supported by the general taxpayer. User charges collected from the registrants are not commensurate with the expenditures required to operate the court. As shown in table 5-5, operating expenses exceed revenues by a factor of nearly five.

As table 5-5 demonstrates, the court is struggling to control expenses against the tide of inflationary pressures. This is difficult because of the fact that the lion's share of its expenditures are from personnel costs associated with experienced professional (legal and engineering) skills. However, despite upward pressures on personnel costs, the court has not increased its basic fees in the last five years.

It should be pointed out that some of the land court's judicial business—estimated at 30 to 40 percent—is attributable to real-estate matters unrelated to registered land. However, this reduction of effort does not apply equally among the entire staff. Approximately half of the staff bears responsibilities devoted exclusively to registered land, and the percentage of time of the remaining half varies with individual responsibilities. Further, some of the revenues

Table 5-5
Land Court Fiscal Summary (1972-1976)

	1976	1975	1974	1973	1972
Expenditures	961,868	979,361	875,039	759,102	682,632
Revenues (excl. assurance fund)	196,488	208,684	200,818	199,604	103,062
Staff positions	62	62	60	59	59

generated by the court are unrelated to land registration. We estimate, therefore, that approximately $625,000 of the $765,000 deficit for 1976 is attributable to operations related to registered land.

User Interests and Concerns

Reasons for Registration

The basic incentives for Massachusetts landowners to register land are threefold. In order of the priorities articulated to us, they are:

1. To clarify title histories or to remove clouds on title;
2. To determine precise boundary lines; and
3. To protect against adverse possession and/or easements by prescription.

We note that these are substantially similar to the reasons offered in the other Torrens jurisdictions. The prime reason for seeking land registration is to obtain a conclusiveness of title and boundary determination that is not otherwise obtainable. To a certain extent, however, the history of land settlement in Massachusetts presents certain unique characteristics relating to title uncertainty that are not present in the other states.

For example, Massachusetts reached a state of fairly comprehensive development earlier than most of the original American colonies. Consequently, most claims of title find their origin in deeds or land grants phrased in the most general of terms. As large tracts were broken into smaller and smaller parcels by transfer and devise throughout the seventeenth and eighteenth centuries, boundary lines were established without the benefit of even the most rudimentary surveying techniques and were commonly described in terms of nonpermanent boundaries such as trees and meandering streams. Along the coastline, the problem was (and is) particularly aggravated by boundary definitions phrased in terms of constantly shifting water lines.

The result is a history of land problems that possibly is common among many of the original colonies. In Massachusetts this history and its associated problems of potentially unmarketable titles and uncertainty over precise boundaries led to the original enactment of the Land Registration Act. Further, it was the experience with boundary problems—an experience that was not present in Illinois and Minnesota because of an early history of extensive surveying—that led to the requirement for the registration of boundaries and the development of the engineering department within the land court. As urban development spread out from the Boston core, land-registration patterns followed in order to secure both the title and boundaries to land.

Persons Using Registration

Because of the peculiar Massachusetts history of title and boundary problems, it is difficult to categorize the more frequent users of the land-registration system. By and large, however, the predominant use patterns are in the direction of commercial and residential development. Unlike the other jurisdictions we examined, there seems to have been little use of the registration system for farmland. In contrast, there has been, and continues to be, substantial use for major office buildings in downtown Boston and for large urban apartment and condominium complexes.

Perhaps the most common users of land registration over the years have been public utilities, residential developers, and promoters of shopping centers, office buildings, industrial parks, and similar complexes.

However, because of the unique boundary-resolution aspects of the Massachusetts system, it might be said that the class of potential users includes almost any landowner who feels the need—aggravated by escalating property values—to perfect both title and boundary determinations. In all cases, we found that the need is directly related to economic incentives. The cost of registration is such that it is only undertaken where the potential for gain is substantial.

This means that there is no specific incentive—thus little actual experience— for the average Massachusetts homeowner to seek land registration. Because of earlier investments by builders and developers, problems relating to title and boundary are inevitably resolved before residential occupancy takes place. As a result, owners of both registered and nonregistered residential property enjoy a problem-free title status that is relatively equal because of efforts undertaken by prior owners.

Impact on Closing Costs

As in the other Torrens jurisdictions, in Massachusetts there is no significant reduction in residential closing costs arising as a result of the property occupying the status of registered land. As indicated earlier, the public registration (filing and processing) fees will be at least $13 higher for registered property. We did find some evidence that registered land can give rise to some reduction in search and examination costs, perhaps as much as 10 to 15 percent ($30 to $50) in some instances. At the same time, we heard much to the contrary from both practicing attorneys and mortgage-lending executives in the Suffolk County area.

We mentioned earlier in this chapter that the prevailing practice in the Boston area with regard to title-assurance mechanisms is for the work to be performed by private attorneys working on the basis of abstracts prepared by themselves or by paraprofessionals employed for that purpose. Mortgage lenders use a variety of methods to engage attorneys to examine the title to the property to be mortgaged. Some use a single law firm exclusively; others allow the borrower to choose from a list of approved attorneys. Still others use several law firms or individual attorneys. In all cases the expenses for this legal work are passed directly through to the buyer at closing.

There is no standard legal fee in the area for title work performed for mortgage lenders. The attorneys we interviewed noted that the tendency over the last five years has been to abandon a flat-rate approach (or one based on a fixed percentage of the amount of the mortgage) in favor of a closer approximation to the services actually performed. At the same time, these attorneys feel they should be entitled to recover increasing amounts relative to the amount of the mortgage—or the value of the property if the work is performed directly for the buyer—because of the increase in liability exposure based on their formal opinion of title.

Focusing on a more or less average transaction involving a $45,000 to $50,000 mortgage, we found that the typical legal fee (involving an uncomplicated residential title) ranges from $300 to $425. We also found that this amount is charged for registered as well as nonregistered land. This fee generally includes preparation of the mortgage documents and attendance at the closing, along with the search, examination, and opinion of title.

Much of the same holds true in cases where the buyer retains an attorney to represent his or her interests in the transaction. Because of the lack of institutional abstracting in the area, the buyer's attorney will assemble his own abstract, or have one prepared, independent of the comparable effort by the lender's attorney. Again, this applies in all cases, without regard to the presence or absence of registered land. And again, the feeling among those interviewed is that the fee will be the same.

The attorneys interviewed indicated that registration status did simplify the process of preparing and assembling the abstract to be examined. They felt, however, that the time saved was relatively insignificant compared with the effort and judgment involved in the analysis and interpretation required to render a sound opinion of title. They also reported that the deed-recording systems in Suffolk and neighboring counties were efficiently maintained, a factor that tends to mitigate any significant difference between registered and unregistered land in the effort required for a thorough search and examination.

The opportunity for even a partial reduction in title-related closing costs because of registered land is directly dependent on the initiative and aggressiveness of prospective home buyers in shopping for mortgage money sources and for legal assistance. Because of fixed policies of many lenders in the area, there will be no opportunity for realizing even a slight reduction in title-related closing expenses, and the buyer of registered residential property will pay the higher registration fees. In those situations where the lender allows the buyer to select the attorney to perform the title work for the lender there may be an opportunity for fee negotiation. However, this opportunity exists for both registered and unregistered property.

Relationship to Title Insurance

We indicated earlier that title insurance is not commonly used in the Boston area for transactions involving residential property. As a matter of custom, the major lenders in the area are content with the use of private attorneys for title assurance and see no particular reason to change. In addition, they generally do not sell mortgage paper on the secondary market. To the contrary, thrift institutions in the area have traditionally been buyers of mortgages from other parts of the country. As a result, they view title insurance as playing a vital role in new construction and in commercial development, but not in the transfer of existing residential property.

There is, therefore, no particular relationship between title insurance and registered homeowner property in the Boston area. Specifically, the assurance fund for registered land is not viewed as interchangeable or competitive, whether in a negative or positive sense, with the insurance coverage offered by title companies. Thus, in the few instances we found where title insurance is required for residential property, no distinction is made for registered land. Conversely, a decision not to seek title insurance is made independent of the registered status of property.

General Observations

The land court is a well-respected institution in Massachusetts. This is clear in opinions expressed in Torrens literature going back to the early part of the century, as well as in opinions of practicing attorneys, law professors, and executives of mortgage lenders and title companies who deal with the court and its work product on a daily basis. Many feel that the unique characteristics of the court—judicial control, statewide jurisdiction, and attention to boundary accuracy—have contributed to its success while Torrens systems have failed in so many other states. Others point to the leadership of a long line of quality judges.

Equally important, we think, is the fact that underlying needs for title clarification and for boundary determination are being met by the registration system. The Massachusetts approach is expensive. However, the incidence of continued registration suggests that landowners with specific needs perceive that the expense is worthwhile. Based upon the opportunity to compare other jurisdictions, we must agree.

It is important, however, to understand the nature of the contributions of the land court. It provides a mechanism to enhance the marketability of land for development purposes by virtue of its capability to eliminate doubts arising from an unclear or potentially damaging history and to settle boundary lines on a basis that is, with few exceptions, legally conclusive. It does not, however, provide a legal framework for title that works to achieve a reduction of residential closing costs. Further, it does not provide an alternative for title insurance in those instances where insurance is deemed important by parties to a land transaction. The assurance fund provided by the registration statute insures against mishaps or errors in the administration of the registration system; it does not insure against risks that are external to the system.

6

Cook County, Illinois

Introduction and Background

Introduction

Illinois enacted the first statutory provisions for land registration in the United States in 1895. In the following year the enactment was ruled unconstitutional by the state supreme court because of the lack of a requirement for a judicial determination of title (*People* v. *Chase*, 165 Ill. 527 (1896)). The initial Illinois statute largely followed the Australian approach, which allowed the registrar—an administrative officer—to make findings with regard to title status and issue certifications regarding conclusiveness of ownership interests.

In 1897, the statute was reenacted with the changes dictated by the *Chase* decision. The new legislation required a judicial determination of title prior to registration. As a result, a second constitutional attack was rejected in the case of *People* v. *Simon*, 165 Ill. 542 (1898). Subsequently, the revised statute was upheld against a series of constitutional attacks, the latest of which involved the decision of the U.S. Supreme Court in *Eliason* v. *Wilborn*, 281 U.S. 457 (1930).

The current version of the Illinois Torrens statute is set forth in Sections 45 through 152 of Chapter 30 of the Illinois Revised Statutes. It is the longest and most detailed of the statutes we have examined—to the point of specifying procedures to be followed in the day-to-day administration of the registrar's office. This is attributable, perhaps, to widespread fears of abuses that might arise from an overly broad delegation of administrative authority.

The Illinois legislation is unique among American land-registration statutes in that its implementation in any county is dependent on adoption by referendum. Since Cook County was the source of the pressure for the legislation, Torrens was adopted there almost immediately after both the 1895 and the 1897 enactments. It is reported, however, that the necessary signatures have been obtained to place the issue on the ballot in only one other county in the state. In 1936 a referendum for the adoption of the Torrens system was defeated in DuPage County, which is situated directly west of Cook County.

Cook County's Torrens system is unique in one other respect. Its historical evolution is traceable to a singular cause—the great Chicago fire of 1871. The county courthouse was burned to the ground during the fire, with the resulting destruction of all real property records. The only creditable land records that survived were those in the offices of three abstracting companies, and many of these files pertained to the downtown area only.

The two decades following the fire were marked by necessary reconstruction as well as rapid expansion of the urban Chicago area. The combined historical records of the abstracting companies that survived the fire were sufficiently complete to meet the title needs for reconstruction of the commercial areas of the original city. However, these records were not complete and in some instances were totally lacking for the expanding areas that previously had been undeveloped. Thus, in the growing part of the city and county, a combination of the lack of both private and public records gave rise to a situation of land unmarketability on a massive scale. A "burnt records act," enacted in 1871 to provide clarification for titles with unclear histories, was considered inadequate because of a required judicial proceeding that proved to be too time consuming for the rapid development taking place.

This was the setting in which the movement for a Torrens system arose. The political pressure for the Illinois legislation was concentrated in a combination of real-estate brokers, developers, and land speculators known as the Cook County Real Estate Board. Their goal was to achieve an expeditious form of title resolution that could fill the void left by the destruction of public records. This need was greatest in the outer parts of the city and county, which were experiencing rapid growth but were seldom the subject of abstracting files because of a lack of prior development. Because of these circumstances, the Cook County Torrens system was used to a much greater extent in the early part of this century than any of the comparable systems established in other states. As a result—despite a noticeable lack of new registrations today—it has the largest number of registered parcels in the county.

Local Real-Estate Customs and Practices

This briefly recited history helps to explain several aspects of land-title practice and circumstances that continue to this day in Cook County.

In the three decades following the establishment of the Torrens system, its sponsors—primarily realtors and developers—used it heavily in furtherance of their interests in promoting continued expansion and development. Professor Powell reported that approximately 21,000 registrations had taken place by 1937, more than for the entire state of Massachusetts over the same period of time. Much of the land involved was farm land or other undeveloped property, which was to be subdivided later. Thus, the number of actual registered parcels was far greater than that revealed by initial registration figures. For example, Powell found that approximately 16 percent of the land transfers filed in Cook County between 1927 and 1936 involved registered land—a percentage slightly higher than we found for the period between 1972 and 1976.

Growth during this period was substantial. The population of the city of Chicago doubled between 1900 and 1930, from 1.7 million to 3.4 million persons. The expansion required by this growth was accompanied by the emergence of two major competing sources for title assurance activity—Torrens and commercial title abstracting and insurance. Each moved from a position of geographic strength occasioned by their respective abilities to fulfill different land-title-related needs. Private abstracting and insurance served the downtown commercial area exclusively—to this day, there is virtually no registered land within "the Loop"—and competed with the public Torrens system for business arising from the rapidly developing outer parts of the city and country. Because of the deficiencies in the public records, private attorneys were not able to conduct their own searches and issue independent opinions of title; instead, they had to rely on commercial abstracts or urge their clients to obtain registration where the land history was inadequate.

As time passed, the lack of pre-1871 public land records became less and less of a barrier to establishing real-estate marketability. By 1931, the conventional deed-recording system reflected the full sixty-year history that some real-estate professionals consider adequate for a reliable title search. However, by this time historical patterns had become well ingrained in the habits of all persons with interests in real estate. Private attorneys, who had little prior experience with the recording system, had grown accustomed to using commercial title services, which had matured from abstracting to guaranty insurance. More important, mortgage lenders became less willing to rely on an attorney's opinion of title based on a commercial abstract and more demanding of complete insurance coverage.

The result is, as a practical matter, that a potential land buyer or mortgage lender seeking title assurance today is presented with two choices—to obtain title insurance or, if the land is already registered, to undertake measures to supplement the features of the Torrens system. Frequently, title insurance will be obtained even if the land is registered. Commercial abstracts of title are not generally available for Cook County property, and it is not common for private attorneys to conduct an independent search and examination of title.

The custom in Cook County is that the seller bears the cost of providing the insurance. This is consistent with the attitude in many other parts of the country that the seller is responsible for producing evidence of good title. In fact, title insurance in Cook County is synonymous with evidence of title. It amounts to a package of services consisting of a search and examination of title and related records, and an inspection of the property, as well as indemnification insurance. In addition, title companies offer closing facilities, escrow services, and a variety of other services related to the enhancement and facilitation of land transactions.

The fact that Cook County is the only county in Illinois to adopt the Torrens system left the state legislature and judiciary in a position similar to that of other states that had never attempted the use of land registration. As a result, Illinois has a well-developed set of "quiet title" proceedings for the resolution of problems giving rise to land-title defects. In addition, Illinois has a marketable title act that extinguishes nonpossessory interests based upon an unrecorded document or occurrence that preexists a forty-year period. Finally, the Cook County recorder/registrar maintains tract indexes for both registered and unregistered land.

In many respects, then, landowners in Cook County have had the opportunity to test virtually all the experiments in land-title reform that American jurisdictions have attempted. On balance, it appears that the Torrens system has not survived the test with the best of grades. In fact, we found the Torrens system to be much in disfavor.

The Torrens Operation

General Description

The Illinois statute reflects a general adherence to the basic Torrens principles followed in other American jurisdictions. Consistent with the constitutional guidelines set forth in early appellate litigation, applications for initial registration are made to the court. The resulting judicial order serves as the authorization for the registrar of titles—the person holding the elective office of recorder of deeds—to register the title and to prepare a certificate in the name of the owner designated in the court order. The statute requires that the office of chief examiner of titles be maintained by the registrar to serve as legal counsel to the registrar and as advisor to the court on registration problems.

The certificate serves as conclusive legal evidence of the ownership of the property described therein. Subject to certain exceptions described in the following section, mortgages, liens, attachments, and other encumbrances or interests affecting the land must be filed with the registrar and entered on the certificate to be legally effective. The result is that prospective purchasers and others interested in the land, or the owner's interest therein, are entitled to rely on the certificate as conclusive of all outstanding claims and interests. It is not possible, for example, for a claimant to establish title by virtue of adverse possession or other form of prescriptive use.

An indemnity fund created from payments assessed at the time of initial registration, and for other services rendered by the registrar, is maintained for the purpose of compensating losses or damages sustained as a result of the initial registration or errors in the subsequent administration of the registration process.

Exceptions

Section 84 of Chapter 30 of the Illinois Revised Statutes provides that a registered owner or bona fide purchaser for value of registered land is legally entitled to rely on the conclusiveness of the status of the title as reflected on the face of the certificate except for:

1. General (county) taxes for the calendar year in which the certificate is issued (at initial registration or subsequently) and special taxes and assessments that have not been confirmed;
2. Liens for internal revenue taxes (U.S.); and
3. Certain appellate rights preserved in the statute (Sections 70-72 and 116) with respect to the initial application for registration or to court-ordered transfers on the death of registered owners.

Section 84 also prescribes a detailed procedure—not found in the other jurisdictions we examined—that requires the registrar to perform separate and distinct tax searches for federal IRS liens and for unpaid general taxes and special taxes and assessments before issuing any certificate of title or entering any new memorial on an existing certificate. The purpose of this procedure, which incurs a statutory fee of $16 ($8 for each search), is to assure that taxes and related governmental claims are kept current. It does not obviate the exceptions specified earlier. That is, current local, state, and federal taxes can be valid claims against the registered property—claims that undercut or dilute the interest of the registered owner—even if they are not disclosed by the special tax searches or do not appear on the official certificate on file with the registrar.

Section 84 also specifies that registered title procured by fraud is not covered by the certification unless the owner claiming on the basis of the certificate is a bona fide purchaser for value who was not a party to or was otherwise unaware of the fraud.

In addition to these statutory exceptions, a series of court decisions and legal interpretations have recognized other, often narrow, exceptions to the conclusiveness of the Torrens certificate. These exceptions include liens, claims, and interests (other than IRS liens) that arise in the name of the state of Illinois or of the United States or that arise from a federal law such as the Bankruptcy Act. Others include leases for a term less than five years (see *Garlick* v. *Imgruet*, 340 Ill. 136 (1930)) and certain implied easements (see *Carter* v. *Michel*, 403 Ill. 610 (1949)). In addition, the Illinois courts, like those of other jurisdictions, have shown a predilection to recognize "equities" in real-property interests that are not consistent with the basic Torrens principle in favor of the conclusiveness of the certificate of title. See, for example, *Echols* v. *Olsen*, 63 Ill. 2d 270 (1976), where a deed from a divorced husband to his ex-wife was improperly filed with the conventional deed records instead of being registered, leaving the official certificate to continue to show both parties as owners. However, the court ordered a subsequent memorialized judgment against the husband to be removed from the certificate, holding that the unregistered deed created an equitable estate in the wife that took priority over the properly registered judgment.

Another important exception to the conclusiveness of the Cook County Torrens certificate arises from an uncertainty that exists as to the applicability of mechanic's liens. Under Illinois law, certain persons accorded the status of mechanics—contractors, subcontractors, and certain suppliers of materials—are entitled to a lien against real property to secure payment for work that has been performed or materials supplied. Further, persons claiming a mechanic's lien are entitled to a period of 120 days in which to perfect their claim. That is, the lien applies against the land from the date of its inception, even though it is not filed/recorded until later in the 120-day statutory time frame.

This conflicts with the basic Torrens requirement that no lien is valid unless and until registered and memorialized on the official certificate. However, no appellate litigation is available to resolve this question. (See, generally, *Chicago and Riverdale Lumber Co.* v. *Vellenga,* 305 Ill. 415 (1922).) Mechanic's liens arise with sufficient frequency, and in significantly large amounts, to make the uncertainty problematic for investors in all instances of new construction. The result is that, as a practical matter, mechanic's liens in Cook County are considered to be a major exception to the conclusiveness of a Torrens title.

Mechanics of Registration

In Cook County, initial registration is accomplished by a judicial proceeding. An application is initiated by filing a petition with the circuit court. Although not required by the statute, the court has a separate land-title division consisting of six judges. However, this division is primarily occupied with real-estate matters unrelated to registered land. Because of the extremely low numbers of initial registrations and the assumption by the chief examiner of the registrar's office of many of the more routine duties formerly referred to the court, only one of the six judges regularly works with registered land.

After receipt of the petition, the case is referred to the chief examiner of titles for examination of title history. In theory, the chief examiner is entitled to examine and certify a privately prepared abstract of title. As a matter of practice, however, the abstracting business is almost nonexistent in Cook County today, and virtually all abstracts are prepared by a unit in the registrar's office that is separate from that of the chief examiner. Pusuant to the examination of the title history, the chief examiner is entitled to hold hearings, examine witnesses, and so forth. In addition, it is required that the property be personally inspected and that any occupancy of the land be ascertained and inquired into. A survey of the property is not required.

The chief examiner's report is made directly to the judge assigned to the case. Legal summons for defendants and notice by publication are required consistent with standard legal procedures. A full trial is available in the event that a defendant or an intervening party elects to contest the application. Legal challenges are rare, however. Typically, the determination of the court is based entirely on the report of the chief examiner. The effect of the final order of the court is to decree the title to the property in the name of the applicant subject to such interests (for example, an outstanding mortgage) recognized in the findings of the court. All other possible claims and interests in the land become legally unenforceable.

A certified copy of the court's order is then filed with the registrar. An official certificate of title to the property is prepared and remains on file with the registrar. Appropriate indexes and documentary cross-references, including a tract index separate from that for unregistered land, are maintained to facilitate the future establishment of easily traceable claims of title. Duplicate certificates are prepared both for owners and mortgagees. Further, the registrar maintains a signature-card file for owners. New owners are required to pick up their duplicates in person, so that their signatures can be obtained as a protection against future forgeries.

Mechanics after Registration

Following initial registration, all interests and claims (other than the exceptions described earlier) that affect the owner's interest in the land, or the status of the title, must be reflected in documents filed with the registrar. A deed authorizing a transfer of ownership must be accompanied by the surrender of the owner's duplicate and results in the cancellation of the existing certificate and the preparation of a new one. Interests in claims that do not disrupt ownership are reflected in memorials entered on the face of the existing certificate. The memorials amount to little more than a brief description of the interests involved. The true legal import arises from the original documents, which are kept on file.

Until registered, legal documents purporting to give rise to interests in land have no legal effect other than that of a contract between the parties to the documents. For example, a deed conveying land from the registered owner to another person continues to function as valid evidence of an enforceable agreement. However, the actual transfer of the ownership interest does not take place until an official certificate is prepared in the name of the new owner. Similarly, a document, such as a mortgage, that creates an interest in the land but does not disturb ownership, is not legally effective against all persons until it is filed and entered as a memorial on the certificate. Subject to the statutory and judicially imposed exceptions, it is the certificate of the registrar that dictates the existence of interests in registered land.

The administrative operation required by the Illinois Torrens Act is similar to that of the other jurisdictions with but a few exceptions. Substantial paper documentation is essential. Further, staffing patterns are required that demand skills appropriate to the interpretation and categorization of legal interests.

A unique feature of the Cook County system is the requirement—in Section 84 of the legislation—that special searches be performed with respect to local taxes and assessments and for IRS liens. Each of these searches must be performed by the registrar before the entry of any new memorial on a certificate, or the issuance of a new certificate. Each costs $8 under the current fee structure, half of which is required by statute to be paid into the indemnity fund. This requirement contributes to a cost structure for administrative processing that is higher than in the other Torrens jurisdictions we examined.

In other respects, the administration of Torrens land in Cook County is subject to requirements for special proceedings adapted to handle recurring situations that are not unlike those in the other jurisdictions. If an owner's or mortgagee's duplicate certificate is lost, the registrar can issue a replacement after inquiry into the circumstances surrounding the loss. The fee for this procedure is $35, an amount set intentionally high in order to encourage careful possession of duplicates.

There are several procedures available for dealing with circumstances arising from the death of registered owners. When joint ownership is involved, the registrar will issue a new certificate in the name of the surviving tenant upon inspection of certain legal documents, that is, the owner's duplicate, the death certificate, an affidavit of the surviving joint tenant, a state inheritance-tax waiver, and a certified copy of the decedent's will. The fee for this procedure is $16.

If joint tenancy is not involved, the transfer of the property (whether by will or intestate distribution) is handled by "transmission" proceedings. If, in accordance with the terms of the decedent's will, the title to the registered land is to be transferred pursuant to a final order of a probate court, the transmission is performed directly by the chief examiner of the registrar's office, who authorizes the issuance of a new certificate. This is a relatively new proceeding intended to relieve the interested parties of the obligation of seeking an order from the land-title division of the court on the basis of an order of the probate court. The chief examiner's office handled 593 proceedings of this type in 1976.

In other cases involving the death of the registered owner, the transmission proceeding is handled by the court. This includes situations where the owner dies without a will, where the executor needs to sell the property pursuant to a power of sale in the will or to satisfy claims against the estate, and where the heirs wish to have the property sold rather than take title themselves. Typically, the court refers these matters to the chief examiner to make specific findings and recommendations back to the court. However, Sections 114 and 115 of the statute require that petitions go to the court in the first instance.

The chief examiner is also obligated to advise the registrar on a wide variety of matters regarding interests in registered land that occur regularly but not necessarily frequently. These include the removal of covenants, conditions, and restrictions memorialized on the certificate, or contained in the certification of title, that are no longer legally effective, the correction of administrative errors in memorials or certificates, transfers of land held in trust, and several other situations involving conservatorships, guardianships, condemnation proceedings, and partition and other judicial decrees. As a general rule, the chief examiner can authorize the registrar to act (that is, enter a memorial or prepare a new certificate) in instances where the legal authority for such action is clearly spelled out. If fact findings are required, if an interpretation of law is involved, or if the chief examiner or registrar refuses to act, the parties at interest must obtain an order from the circuit court.

The Indemnity Fund

Sections 136 and 137 of Chapter 30 of the Illinois Revised Statutes require the establishment of a county fund. This fund is described in the statute as an "indemnity" fund. It does not appear, however, that the selection of this term over that of "assurance" used by the other jurisdictions has any particular significance. The purpose of the fund—to compensate for losses sustained as a result of the Torrens operation—remains the same. A significant difference in Cook County exists by virtue of the size of the fund; its year-end 1975 value was in excess of $4 million.

Fund Administration

The fund is generated by the assessment of a fee in the amount of two-tenths of one percent ($2 per $1,000) of the value of the property, which is collected at the time of (1) initial registration; (2) transfer of the land by devise or descent upon the death of a registered owner; and (3) issuance of a new certificate to a purchaser at a tax sale. The fee was doubled by a 1975 amendment to the legislation. Formerly, it was the same rate (one-tenth of one percent) used in Massachusetts and Minnesota.

The determination of property valuation is made by the registrar, whose policy is to observe the assessed value established for tax purposes. As a general rule, Cook County assesses real estate used as a farm or for residential purposes improved with not more than six living units at 17 percent of fair market value.

An additional source of revenue for the indemnity fund arises from the requirement for the two tax searches that must be performed by the registrar before any memorial is entered on a certificate or a new certificate is issued. The Illinois statute requires that half ($4) of the $8 charge for each search be paid into the indemnity fund.

The fees assessed for the fund are collected by the registrar's office and paid to the county treasurer, who is required to invest the fund. Investments are restricted by Section 137 of the statute to bonds and securities of the United States, of the state of Illinois, or of counties or municipalities of the state. All investments require the approval of the circuit court. The effect of these provisions, in combination with the supervisory responsibility of the court, is to segregate the fund from other assets of the county.

The wording of the statutory provisions relating to the fund is not clear as to whether other assets of the county are available for claims settlement in the event that the fund is exhausted. Section 138 specifies that a civil action for a claim can be brought against the county. And Section 139 states: "Until the indemnity fund provided as aforesaid shall have been exhausted, payment for any such losses or damages shall be made out of such fund." The chief examiner interprets this language to mean that the Illinois legislature intended county assets to stand behind the fund. Those who disagree rely on the lack of any specific language to that effect and a court decision in Nebraska (see *Jones* v. *York County*, 26 F. 2d 56 (1928)). As a practical matter, the size of the fund seems to have partially mitigated some of the concerns investors have about this unclarity.

As of November 30, 1975—the end of the county's 1975 fiscal year—the value of the Cook County indemnity fund stood at $4 million. This includes approximately $255,000 earned from investments that year and $111,500 in income from fees collected by the registrar. Since the fees attributable to the fund were doubled beginning in January 1976, the chief examiner estimates that the annual contributions should exceed $220,000 a year on the basis of average volumes. Because of the very low number of current initial registrations, most of this income is generated from transfers of land resulting from the death of registered owners and from tax searches.

Claims Management

The fund is available for compensation for losses sustained as a result of errors in initial registration as well as from subsequent administration of the land. The latter includes omissions and mistakes by the registrar's office. Claims can be presented directly to the county board (the legislative body for the county) or brought in the circuit court against the county. A judicial appeal from an adverse decision of the board is provided.

As of 1936, Professor Powell reported that a total of $17,035 had been paid from the indemnity fund. Since that time, many claims have been brought and paid from the fund. In 1975, fourteen claims were presented and paid in a total amount of $15,222.35. The largest was $3,300 and the smallest was $55. In thirteen of the fourteen, the claimant was the county tax collector; in the other, the claimant was the county clerk.

The chief examiner of the registrar's office reports that this is about average. The overwhelming majority of the claims are for unpaid taxes, arising from errors (omissions) in the execution of the tax searches performed by the registrar's office. In the past, there have been claims arising from other kinds of errors and from fraud perpetrated by persons who gained possession of the owner's duplicate.

However, the chief examiner asserts that there has never been a claim based on the improper cutoff of a property interest at the time of initial registration.

It is not clear under the statute whether a party claiming loss is entitled to include legal and other costs incidental to the prosecution of the claim. There is no reported litigation on the point. The effect is softened somewhat by the fact that a claimant is entitled to apply directly to the board without undertaking litigation. Section 137 of the statute requires the board to seek the advice of the registrar as to each claim presented. The policy of the chief examiner is to expedite the processing of claims whenever possible. However, this does not relieve a potential claimant of the burden of seeking independent legal assistance.

We encountered some concern among local real-estate interests for the fact that the legislative status of the county board might inject political considerations into the claim-evaluation procedure. There are rumors, but no real evidence, of this happening in the 1920s and 1930s. Further, we found no awareness of any recent example of abuses of this kind and no reported litigation relevant to the point.

Economic Considerations

Frequency and Extent of Registration

The chief examiner of the registrar's office estimates that 28.5 percent, or 370,500 of the approximately 1.3 million parcels of land in the county are registered. This estimate is based on the number of owner's signature cards maintained by the office, which exceed 500,000, with allowances made for repetition because of joint ownership.

Analysis of the annual transaction volumes of the office suggests that the

28.5 percent estimate may be too high. As table 6-1 demonstrates, the number of recorded transfers and mortgages for Torrens land consistently averages in the neighborhood of 15 percent of the total number of transactions handled by the recorder/registrar's office. We are inclined to think, therefore, that an estimate of 18 to 20 percent (or approximately 234,000 to 260,000 parcels) is a more accurate reflection of the incidence of registered land in Cook County.

Further, the incidence of new land registration has been undergoing a steady and rapid decline. In the last ten years, initial applications have dropped, from forty in 1966 to three in 1976. Table 6-2 shows this pattern of decline. In addition, the average value attributed to each application—computed by dividing the total value by the number of applications—reveals that parcels going into land registration are not large. This suggests that the more recent registrations do not represent land that will be subdivided into far greater numbers of registered parcels.

On the average there have been only sixteen applications for registration each year during the last decade. This is a far cry from the period between 1915 and 1925, when the annual number of applications averaged well in excess of a thousand. The lack of incentives for continued registrations is discussed later. In the context of the immediate discussion, it is important to note that, while initial registrations have declined to the point of practical insignificance, the number of registered parcels continues to grow. Historically, much of the land that went into registration was farmland and other undeveloped property in the outlying parts of the county. Today, these previously registered tracts are becoming an increasingly important source of land available for development.

Cost of Initial Registration

The cost of initial registration in Cook County is comparable to that found in the Twin Cities area, but substantially below that in Massachusetts. At a

Table 6-1
Real-Estate Transfers in Cook County (1972-1976)

	Total Transfers	Total Mortgages[a]	Torrens Transfers	Percent of Total	Torrens Mortgages[a]	Percent of Total
1972	82,321	99,765	13,908	16.9	15,316	15.4
1973	85,182	98,724	13,499	15.8	14,879	15.1
1974	69,605	81,001	9,939	14.3	11,584	14.3
1975	66,951	87,463	9,650	14.4	12,544	14.3
1976	83,089	102,801	12,866	15.5	15,259	14.8

[a]Includes trust deeds.

Table 6-2
Applications for Initial Registration (Cook County, 1966-1976)

	Number	Total Value	Average Value
1966	40	$ 989,000	$ 24,725
1967	38	1,978,700	52,071
1968	26	1,556,800	59,877
1969	16	620,600	38,788
1970	17	301,500	18,844
1971	14	343,500	24,536
1972	12	402,000	33,500
1973	21	509,500	24,262
1974	7	795,400	113,629
1975	9	612,500	68,056
1976	3	225,000	75,000

minimum, the consensus among the lawyers we interviewed was that probable expenses were in the neighborhood of $575 to $775 and that the time required was approximately six months. These estimates are based on assumptions as to the lack of contest against the application and the absence of problems that might give rise to special requirements.

Table 6-3 itemizes the costs that would be encountered in a typical registration. For purposes of the fee assessed for the indemnity fund, we have assumed an assessed property valuation of $25,000. The abstract is prepared by the registrar's office; the $115 is an estimate of average cost provided by the chief examiner.

Table 6-3
Cook County Initial Registration Costs

Abstract preparation	$115
Circuit court fee	15
Registrar's fee	30
Public advertising	26
Summons	2
Federal lien search	8
State tax search	8
Registration of decree	10
Certificate	10
Indemnity fund fee	50
Attorney's fee	300 (to 500)
Total	$574 (to 774)

The major variable of the various cost components for registration is that for legal services. All other cost components are public charges, and all but the court fee arise from the registrar's office. For the most part, these costs are independent of the value or the size of the property involved. The only cost directly dependent on value is the fee for the indemnity fund.

Cost of Subsequent Activity

After the initial registration, the owner or subsequent buyer of Torrens property incurs expenses in the form of public fees (from the registrar's office) for the acceptance and entry of routine documents relating to transfer or to other legal incidents affecting the land, which are substantially higher than those for nonregistered property. In addition, costs in the form of public fees, and occasionally attorney's fees, arise from circumstances incurring costs that are unique to Torrens land.

The common registration and recording fees for Torrens and unregistered land are set forth in table 6-4. This fee schedule adequately depicts the differential involved in a typical sale of residential property. The fees for nonregistered land will total $30—for the recording of the deed, the release of the seller's mortgage, and the buyer's new mortgage. If Torrens land is involved, the same transaction will cost $76—the same charges for the three documents, plus charges for the issuance of a new certificate, for the mortgagee's duplicate, for the entry of the memorial showing the new mortgage, and for the conduct of the two tax searches.

Table 6-4
Cook County Registrar/Recorder Fees

	Torrens	*Nonregistered*
Deeds	$10	$10
Issuing certificate	10	N/A
Mortgages	10	10
Entering memorial	10	N/A
Other instruments (e.g., mortgage release)	10	10
Canceling memorial	5	N/A
Mortgagee's duplicate	10	N/A
Tax search	8	N/A
Federal lien search	8	N/A

The foregoing reflects charges at the time of the transfer itself. Common mortgage practice in Cook County dictates that the two tax searches be performed prior to the time of the mortgage commitment at a cost of another $16, together with the obtaining of a certified copy of the seller's certificate (for purposes of examination)—for still another $10. Further, it is common that the release of the seller's mortgage is not available as of the time of closing. If this happens, there is a break in the simultaneity of the title transfer. The deed and new mortgage will be filed and the proceeds of the new mortgage loan held in escrow. Even if the release of the old mortgage is filed one day later, another set of tax searches is required to be performed (for another $16) and yet another certificate prepared (for still another $10). Thus, it is not unusual for the registrar's fees to total $128 for a typical residential transfer—compared to $30 for the same transaction for unregistered land.

In other respects, the fee schedule of the registrar is somewhat less onerous in terms of direct landowner impact. As discussed in an earlier section, a combination of statutory and administrative policies has evolved over the years to allow the chief examiner to authorize the issuance of a new certificate in the event of a lost duplicate or in such cases as changes in trust terms or transmission proceedings in the event of the death of a registered owner, or to direct the removal of obsolete or erroneous memorials. There is no charge for these quasi-judicial services. However, these occurrences inevitably involve registration fees (for example, $20 for filing a new document and issuance of a new certificate). The fees for replacement of a lost owner's or mortgagee's duplicate certificate total $35.

In addition, many of these legal occurrences require the assistance of an attorney. Some, in fact, grow out of a context in which an attorney is already involved, as in the case of the probate of a registered owner's will. However, even the most routine cases rarely involve less than two to three hours of an attorney's time. Thus, at a reported hourly rate in the Chicago area of $40, we estimate that many of these proceedings will cost a registered landowner an additional $80 to $120.

Cost of Administration

Prior to January 1, 1976, the Torrens division of the Cook County recorder registrar's office was operating at a substantial net loss. Direct personnel expenditures alone almost doubled revenues gathered. Additional costs for expenditures for administrative and support services (supplies, materials, maintenance, and the like) increased the size of the deficit substantially. This meant that the Torrens division was dependent on excess revenues generated by the conventional recording division.

As of January 1, 1976, however, the fee schedule for both the Torrens and the conventional recording divisions was doubled. Table 6-5 illustrates the impact of the doubling of fees during fiscal year 1976 (ending November 30) and includes the county comptroller's budget projections for 1977. While the office as a whole had an excess of revenues over expenses that was close to $5 million in 1976, it appears that the Torrens division continued to show a deficit once allowance was made for its share of administrative and support services. If the comptroller's 1977 projections hold true, this deficit seems bound to increase.[a]

Further, it is important to note that the increased expenditures involved are dictated by the nature of the Torrens system, which requires a significant increase over conventional recording in both the numbers and the quality of skilled personnel. Comparison of the 1976 budget shows that the conventional recording operation requires a staff of 81 persons, whereas the Torrens operation, which handles less than one-fourth of the activity, requires 134. Further,

Table 6-5
Cook County Registrar/Recorder Financial Data

	Torrens Division	Recording Division[a]	Totals
1975 Actual			
Revenues	$ 783,910	$3,806,122	$4,590,023
Personnel costs	$1,574,202	$ 868,035	$2,442,237
Admin./support costs	N/A	N/A	$ 946,716
Personnel assigned	137	88	308
1976 Actual			
Revenues	$1,700,774	$6,461,940	$8,162,714
Personnel costs	$1,571,943	$ 877,254	$2,449,297
Admin./support costs	N/A	N/A	$ 944,588
Personnel assigned	134	81	303
1977 Projected			
Revenues	$1,683,000	$6,067,000	$7,750,000
Personnel costs	$1,816,207	$ 959,122	$2,775,329
Admin./support costs	N/A	N/A	$1,163,140
Personnel assigned	134	81	303

[a]Figures include some revenues and personnel assigned to UCC filings and other functions unrelated to land records.

---

[a]This is confirmed by a 1978 bill introduced in the Illinois legislature to increase the Cook County registrar's fee for initial registration from $30 to $1,000. The purpose offered in support of the bill is to reduce deficits.

the average annual salary for the recording division is $10,830, compared with $11,732 for the Torrens division.

User Interests and Concerns

Reasons for Registration

Earlier we noted that initial registrations in Cook County have steadily decreased to the point of nonexistence. In 1976 only three new applications were filed. This is contrary to the experience in Massachusetts and Minnesota. While we noted some decline in initial registrations in the latter jurisdictions, we also noted a shift in the pattern of usage. In both areas, new registrations tended to follow the spread of residential development toward the outer fringe of the metropolitan area. At the same time, landowners pursuing commercial development within the urban core continue to use registration as dictated by conditions suggesting unmarketability of title.

This has not happened in Cook County. To the contrary, we found an inclination on the part of lawyers to avoid registration if at all possible. For example, the chapter on the Torrens system in *Basic Real Estate Practice*, a professional handbook published by the Illinois Institute for Continuing Legal Education in 1976, characterizes nineteen attributes of the system as problems and nine as benefits (see pages 7-19 through 7-23). In fact, we found that lawyers who work with developers were interested in a legal change that would permit their clients to withdraw land from registration. The only reason we were offered for initiating new registrations is to resolve the dilemma arising from the combination of a registered and an unregistered parcel of land. Since registered land cannot be deregistered, the only method available to simplify a combined parcel is to integrate it into a single registered unit.

The lawyers we interviewed were real-estate specialists practicing in downtown Chicago. All had considerable experience with the Torrens system. None was particularly positive about Torrens; most were negative. For the most part, the negative feelings relayed to us arose from experiences with the administration of the operation.

Several reasons explain this reaction:

1. First, and perhaps foremost, is the particular history supporting the development of the system. The Cook County Torrens system was created to deal with a unique situation—widespread title unmarketability that existed during a period of rapid growth and development because of the loss of land records from the Chicago fire. This underlying rationale has long since ceased to justify a continuing incidence of new registrations. The use of land registration began a pattern of steady decline in the 1930s once the lack of pre-1871 records began to have diminishing practical and legal significance.

2. Since Torrens was confined to Cook County only, the Illinois legislature and judiciary were required to develop legal mechanisms that met needs for clarification of title and elimination of defects, which were available statewide. Examples are a marketable title act and a well-developed set of quiet-title procedures. Consequently, Cook County landowners have had the opportunity to choose non-Torrens sources of relief from land-title problems unrelated to the destruction of records during the great fire.

3. The Cook County Torrens operation has been handicapped by the difficulties in staffing patterns associated with many public offices. This appears to have contributed to administrative problems, which, in turn have encouraged landowners to seek alternative sources of relief. Since the Torrens operations is a creature of statutory direction and local budgetary constraints, it lacks both the flexibility and the economic resources to recruit and maintain the personnel required to fulfill landowner needs for operational regularity and dependability.

Persons Using Registration

As indicated in the prior section, persons seeking land registration today are almost nonexistent. Historically, Torrens was heavily used in Cook County by residential developers and for farms and other underdeveloped land. It was rarely used by owners and developers of major commercial property. While Cook County may have as many as 260,000 registered parcels of land—a number that probably exceeds that of the urban areas of Boston, Minneapolis, and St. Paul combined—there is virtually no registered land in the downtown Chicago business/financial area known as "the Loop." Further, it appears from the ratio of land transfers illustrated in table 6-6 that a greater percentage of registered land lies outside the city than within.

Table 6-6
Cook County Land Transfers by Municipal Status

	1975		1976	
	Torrens	*Unregistered*	*Torrens*	*Unregistered*
Within Chicago	3,328	23,936	2,838	27,149
Outside Chicago	9,538	33,365	6,812	43,074
Totals	12,866	57,301	9,650	70,223

This is explained by the historical role Torrens has played in meeting landowner needs in Cook County. Since a great deal of the central core of Chicago had already been rebuilt by the time of the introduction of Torrens, land-title histories had been reestablished, private abstract records were considered adequate, and there were no perceived advantages in using the new system. In contrast, the sponsors of the system were interested in the development of land in the outer parts of the city and the rest of the county, where private abstract records were incomplete and histories were unclear because of reduced activity since the fire. It was precisely this land that went into registration in large volumes during the period between 1900 and 1930.

In those early years there were clear economic incentives—in addition to the advantage of securing title clarification—for residential developers to use Torrens. Because of the custom that sellers bear the cost of providing evidence of title marketability, it was cheaper for developers to absorb the cost for a single registration and a certificate for each unit than to provide the title abstract and/or insurance for each unit in the development. Over time, however, these economies have disappeared.

Residential developers continue to use registered land today only because much of the land available for development is already registered. For a variety of reasons, they have become unwilling to make any new applications. One set of factors recited to us is distinctly economic. Another relates to uncertainties and problems encountered in dealing with the registrar's office. Still a third arises from what is perceived as the inflexibility of the Torrens system—its inability, because of statutory limits, lack of administrative discretion, or operational considerations, to deal promptly with particular situations.

One example, offered to us as fairly typical, illustrates these factors. Under current construction practices it is not uncommon for a developer to go through several mortgages before the construction is complete. When the subdivision is filed, a certificate will be prepared for each unit. Each successive mortgage incurred by the developer will incur registration charges for each unit certificate. For example, the release of a prior mortgage and the substitution of a new one requires fees totalling $30 for each unit—$10 for each document, plus $10 for the entry of the memorial reflecting the new mortgage. Thus, a fifty-unit subdivision could incur $1,500 in registration fees each time new financing is obtained. Further fees would be required at the time of each sale for releases of the outstanding mortgages. In addition, developers find that investor concern over the possibility of mechanic's liens in all cases of new construction manifests itself in a requirement for title insurance. Thus, a developer in Cook County finds that Torrens land produces no freedom from the obligation of providing title insurance and frequently requires significant extra expenses, which are not always predictable in advance.

The problem appears even worse where condominiums are involved. Illinois law requires that a "declaration of condominium" (the functional equivalent of

a subdivision plan) be supported by a survey. However, a survey cannot be performed until construction is completed. Thus, the Torrens office has taken the
position that a deed to a particular unit cannot be accepted (and a certificate
issued) until the survey has been filed. In turn, the lender to a unit purchaser
who buys in advance of construction completion will insist that the loan proceeds (and supporting deeds and mortgages) be held in escrow until registration
can be accomplished. This can be costly for the developer who is paying over 10
percent interest and is unable to gain access to thousands of dollars of sales
proceeds. One attorney related two separate experiences in which over $1 mil-
lion was held in escrow because of the inability of the registrar's office to accept
a deed.

The instances related have obvious economic repercussions. They are also
instances that—together with time delays in issuing new certificates or even in
accepting documents for filing during peak periods—give rise to perceptions of
Torrens phrased in terms of bureaucracy, administrative rigidity, and the like.
The problems described do not arise in the other jurisdictions we examined. The
result is that lawyers, developers, investors, and others with interests in Cook
County real estate have tended to avoid the Torrens system whenever possible.

Impact on Closing Costs and Title Insurance

Because title insurance is the accepted method in Cook County for search and
examination of title history, the analysis of the impact of Torrens on this
aspect of closing costs necessarily involves a direct comparison with title insurance. This is unfortunate for several reasons. As discussed in chapter 3, the
two are not directly comparable. That part of a title policy which provides
insurance protection applies to title-related risks that are not covered by the
Torrens certificate and indemnity fund. In Illinois, the most obvious examples
are mechanic's liens and claims based on federal law.

Further, title insurance affords protection from important but non-title-
related risks, which Torrens in Cook County cannot offer; examples are questions of survey, the existence of parties in possession, or unconfirmed special
assessments of local municipalities.

The reality is that Torrens protection and private insurance protection
are not mutually exclusive. In virtually all instances involving new construction, Cook County mortgage lenders need title insurance because of problems
with mechanic's liens. In addition, lenders anticipating the sale of mortgage
obligations into the secondary market need title insurance to satisfy the requirements of institutional investors. The result is that a significant number
of Cook County residential transactions involving Torrens land are closed
through the vehicle of title insurance. Figures provided us by the Chicago Title
and Trust Company, which has a substantial part of the business in the county,

show that this one company insured a total of 1,833 of the 12,866 Torrens transfers in 1976 and 2,059 of 9,650 in 1975. Thus, in what may be as much as 25 percent of Torrens closings, title-related costs include title insurance as well as Torrens charges. In these cases, the closing costs include the additional registration charges together with the expense of title insurance.

In those Torrens transactions which are not transferred pursuant to title insurance, we found that until recently the opportunity for realizing a saving in closing costs existed primarily in the case of more expensive housing. In a typical transaction there was some, but little, saving if the buyer did not obtain private legal representation. In fact, the exclusively Torrens transaction cost more for moderately priced housing. This is attributable to the fact that Torrens charges are fixed without regard to the sale price of the property. Earlier, the pricing structure of most title insurance in the area offered a reissue rate that substantially reduced the cost of coverage if the property had been insured earlier by the same company.

Under the insurance rate schedules that currently prevail, however, the insured residential transaction involving unregistered land can cost as much as $100 more in closing costs than a comparable transaction involving noninsured registered land. For example, assuming a transaction for the sale of an existing residence at a price of $50,000, the cost to the seller of fulfilling the customary obligations of furnishing title insurance to the buyer is $222. To this sum must be added $50 for mortgagee coverage—a separate policy running to the benefit of the lender, which we assume would be required of the buyer—and $30 in recording fees. Thus, the total title-related closing costs in an insured, but unregistered, $50,000 residential transaction would be $302.

In comparison, the charges for the equivalent transaction involving uninsured Torrens land will average $193 to $204, plus any attorney fee incurred by the buyer. This amount is computed by adding a $65 to $80 estimated fee for an independent survey of the property to the $76 in registration fees explained in the prior section (see table 6-3), plus $16 for tax searches ordered by the lender at the time of commitment, and yet another $36 for the typical situation where the release of the prior mortgage was not available to be filed simultaneously with the deed and the new mortgage.

The survey requirement is uniformly imposed by those lenders who elect to rely on the Torrens system to the exclusion of privately issued title insurance. It is not a full-scale survey. Rather, it is a brief inspection of the property accompanied by a "quick sketch" designed to show whether improvements are within the proper boundaries. The equivalent service is provided by title companies for both registered and unregistered land and is included within the rate quoted for insurance coverage.

Lenders who are content to rely on the Torrens system without pursuing private insurance coverage satisfy their needs for title protection by examination of the official certificate. Typically, inspection is made of a certified copy of the certificate provided by the seller. The examination will be made by a lawyer or other specially trained person employed by the lender. Although this involves an extra step in the loan processing, one not required for unregistered land, the lenders we interviewed did not impose a separate charge for this examination process.

Finally, if the parties to a residential transfer elect to retain private legal representation, there appears to be an unquantifiable impact on the amount of legal fees that runs to the detriment of the Torrens buyer. Since the custom in the area is that the seller provides title insurance to the buyer, lawyers do not generally undertake an independent search and examination of the title to insured property. Mortgage lenders as well as lawyers for the buyer and for the seller rely on the commitment of the title company as evidence of good title.

If Torrens land is involved, the main concern of the seller's attorney is to make a certified copy of the offered certificate available to the lender of the buyer and, usually, a photocopy thereof to the buyer's attorney. The attorney will assuredly examine the copy and will visit the registrar's office prior to closing to inspect the original. This effort may be a small matter for the downtown attorney with offices only minutes away from the registrar. However, for suburban attorneys—who practice in the communities with the majority of registered land—the trip downtown may consume as much as an hour in travel time each way. The extra time involved naturally invites additional legal fees. Since the time and the fees vary, we cannot accurately estimate the true costs involved. The effect, however, can be to bring the title-related costs for Torrens property fairly close to those for title insurance. In addition, the Torrens buyer (and mortgage lender) ends up assuming some risks that would be covered by title insurance.

General Observations

It is apparent from our interviews that the Torrens system in Cook County is not accorded the degree of respect from real-estate professionals that its counterparts enjoy in Massachusetts and Minnesota. In several places in this chapter, we have suggested various reasons that contribute to this result. We think the predominant reason is the lack of any tangible incentives. The costs that Torrens entails—both in ascertainable time and dollars and in subsequent unexpected demands—are not perceived as worthy of its potential benefits. Considering the fact that the direct costs of initial registration are consistent with those in the Twin Cities area and considerably cheaper than those in Massachusetts, we can only conclude that the underlying need that attracts landowners to registration in these other jurisdictions—to remove clouds on title associated with an uncertain history—is not compelling in Cook County today.

To a certain extent, the attitudes about Torrens we encountered are colored by misgivings about the day-to-day administration of the registrar's office. We regularly encountered concern about delays, administrative failings, inflexibility, and trouble in general. An example is the fact that in the spring of 1977, the office was twenty-three weeks behind in the delivery of duplicate certificates. To the credit of the office, the chief examiner and his legal staff are well respected. We found much awareness of the complaints, and measures were under way to deal with them constructively—in the form of proposed new legislation and an upgrading of equipment and facilities. At the same time, the office is handicapped by fairly typical governmental constraints—salaries are low, employee turnover is high, and it is difficult to plan for the kinds of upturns in activity represented by the one-third increase in volume in 1976 over 1975.

We are inclined to conclude, however, that an upgrading in administrative capabilities would not bring about a substantial change in attitudes among real-estate professionals. Torrens was created in Cook County to deal with a unique set of needs occasioned by the Chicago fire. The title problems attributable to this history gave rise to the registration of large numbers of land parcels in the years between 1900 and 1930. Since that time, the underlying historical pressures have dissipated. No particular incentives are available to attract new registrations. Thus, the main function of the system today is to administer the land that was registered by prior generations of landowners.

7

Related Experiences

In addition to on-site examination of the Torrens systems in Massachusetts, Minnesota, and Cook County, Illinois, we examined the literature available on the other American jurisdictions that attempted the Torrens approach. With the exception of Hawaii's statewide system, these experiments, involving perhaps more than two hundred counties, must be considered failures. Since seventeen different states were involved, representing all parts of the country, this experience suggests conclusions that can be drawn relative to the need for land registration in the United States generally.

We also examined the experience with compulsory registration in Great Britain. Here, we were struck by the difficulties in making meaningful comparisons. However, the legal systems are not dissimilar and the original difficulties Britain had in implementing land registration (despite the lack of a preexisting recording system) are comparable to many American experiences. Thus, the subsequent time and expense involved in achieving compulsory registration, *without* achieving any reduction in residential closing costs, seem relevant.

Finally, we reviewed the developments related to the automation of land-record-keeping functions. The theoretical arguments look good; yet the actual developments are some years removed from proving the potential that might exist realistically. There is insufficient experience available to draw any conclusions about the value that automation holds for land-records systems. In any case, questions concerning automation are separate and distinct from the desirability of land registration. There is an unfortunate recurring confusion between the two subject areas in much of the current literature.

Other American Jurisdictions

Altogether, twenty-one states attempted the Torrens approach. Much of the original legislation was enacted in an eleven-year period, between 1896 and 1907. This activity led to the development of a Uniform Land Registration Act by the National Conference of Commissioners on Uniform State Laws. The uniform model brought about enabling legislation in six states, four of which—Mississippi (1914), South Carolina (1916), Tennessee (1917), and Utah (1917)—repealed the authorization within fifteen years because of lack of use. Also under the influence of the development of the Uniform Act, Pennsylvania adopted a constitutional amendment authorizing land registration in 1915, but never succeeded in enacting the necessary legislation.

Of the remaining sixteen states, three—Massachusetts, Minnesota, and Illinois—are covered in detail in the preceding chapters. The experiences of another nine states are briefly discussed in this chapter. The other four states— Nebraska, North Dakota, South Dakota, and Virginia—are not discussed because there are few data available except for the fact of almost nonexistent usage. The histories available in the general literature indicate that the political support for Torrens in those states was largely from farming organizations. Considering that the actual experience with land registration proved to be an almost exclusively urban phenomenon, it is perhaps not surprising that the original expectations were not realized in the more rural states.

The conclusion that can be drawn from these different experiments with Torrens is that it never really took hold. Despite the initial enthusiasm for the theoretical concept (manifested in the Torrens enactments), the actual number of registrations was almost always small. For the most part, by the early 1920s, the incidence of registrations had already subsided in those counties which had any prior experience. It is as if the only land appropriate for, or in need of, registration was identified and selected out for special legal treatment in less than a single generation.

Hard data on the use patterns in many of these states are available in five distinct surveys performed years ago. While there are obvious biases in some of these works, there is little difference as to actual statistics. The first appears in the 1922 edition of the *Journal of Law and Banking*. The second, done by Professor McCall, is published in the 1932 *North Carolina Law Review*. The remaining three were performed in the mid-thirties at approximately the same time. One was a state-by-state federal WPA survey occasioned by the interest of the federal Home Owners Loan Corporation in exploring alternatives helpful for the reestablishment of the collapsed housing market. Another was undertaken by a practicing San Francisco attorney, Mr. Edward Landels. The last was done by Professor Powell and is referred to several times in this book. Although ostensibly concerned with New York, the Powell study is the most comprehensive data source on the other experiences. While Powell drew on the earlier studies, he also surveyed each of the states independently. His study—now forty years old—is the most recent thorough review of Torrens in the United States.

California

California first enacted Torrens legislation in 1897. There was little use of its provisions and it was replaced by a new and more comprehensive statute in 1915, which, among other things, established a single statewide insurance fund. Meanwhile, the state enacted a burnt records act (referred to as the McEnerney Act) in 1906 providing an expeditious nonregistration judicial procedure for establishing clear title. This statute was occasioned by the loss by fire of public records during the San Francisco earthquake (see *American Land Co.* v. *Zeiss,* 219 U.S. 47 (1911)).

The experience with Torrens following the 1915 statute was almost exclusively confined to the four counties in Southern California—Los Angeles, Orange, San Bernadino, and San Diego Counties. The Powell study cites WPA and other data showing that by 1935 fewer than 300 parcels of land had been registered in the rest of the state and practically none in urban San Francisco. However, even in the four southern counties the use of registration was not high. The largest, Los Angeles County, had nearly 9,000 registered parcels, which represented less than one percent of the total parcels in the county.

Apparently, the administration of the Torrens system—especially in Los Angeles—was extremely poor. This led to a series of court decisions that unavoidably undermined the legal reliability of the certificates. A 1927 federal court judgment, *Gill* v. *Frances Investment Co.,* 19 F.2d 880 (1927), eventually resulted in a $48,000 claim that left the nearly $40,000 statewide insurance fund with a deficit of over $8,000. This brought an end to new registrations in California.

Confronted with a bankrupt fund and little opportunity to replenish it because of a lack of new registrations, the California legislature authorized the withdrawal of land from registration in 1949. Withdrawals ran so high, particularly in Los Angeles, that a study was commissioned to review the situation. A comprehensive review of Torrens led to the repeal of the statute in 1955.

Colorado

Enacted in 1903, the Colorado Torrens provisions were little used in many parts of the state. The available literature agrees that the major impetus for the original statute was problems with titles in the nonmountainous eastern part of the state. Homesteader abandonment of farms because of drought, and foreclosures and tax liens resulting from financial failures in the 1890s, created a need for an expeditious means for clarifying ownership status. Accordingly, much of the land registered in Colorado is in these rural counties. Even so, the data available indicate that the incidence of registration was still low in this area.

We were unable to locate precise data on the use of Torrens in the heavily populated and rapidly growing "front range" area of Colorado, centered by Denver. While registration systems were established in most of the counties comprising this area, it appears that they are rarely used today. Perhaps less than one percent of the land in these counties is registered.

Georgia

Georgia enacted a modified version of the Uniform Land Registration Act in 1917. It appears that little use was made of its provisions. The only serious attempt is reported to have been in the southeastern corner of the state, involving large acreage tracts of undeveloped timber and swamp land. The apparent motivation was to protect the title from adverse possession by squatters. The available data indicate that the use of registration was rare in the more populated areas of the state.

From the beginning, the Georgia legislation allowed withdrawal from registration by a simple filing by the registered owner. The lack of information indicating any current registration activity suggests that most of the land initially registered has been subsequently withdrawn.

Hawaii

Hawaii authorized land-title registration in 1903. The law is derived from that of Massachusetts and establishes a statewide system operated by a central land court. Initially, the statute required compulsory registration of any land owned by a corporation. This provision was stricken in 1907, but it had the effect of bringing into registration large tracts of undeveloped land, much of it in the form of agricultural plantations on the smaller islands.

A major incentive for title registration in Hawaii was the avoidance of confusion arising from native property-law concepts. This apparently attracted the interest of large property investors. The Powell study reports that banks adopted policies requiring registration for all loans involving property lacking clear record title. This undoubtedly contributed to making the Hawaiian land court one of the few surviving Torrens systems in the United States.

The currently available data indicate that something in the neighborhood of 25 percent of the land parcels in Honolulu are registered and that one or more of the less-populated islands that comprise the state may have close to 50 percent. It seems clear that much of the land involved was placed into registration decades ago. However, we were not able to identify the nature and extent of new registrations in the post-World War II expansion and development that led to statehood status.

New York

Although it is one of the lesser of the many infrequent users of land registration, New York's experience with Torrens is significant because of the presence of the largest urban area in the country. Its initial enactment occurred in 1908 after several years of pressure from real-estate brokers and developers in the New York City area. Almost nonexistent usage thereafter led to a series of statutory amendments, culminating in a comprehensive revision in 1918.

The Powell study found that by 1937 there were no registrations in over two-thirds of the counties in the state and very few in the rest. Surprisingly, little use had been made in the five-county New York City area, with even less in the other counties. The greatest use was in Suffolk County (on Long Island), largely by speculators who acquired title originally from tax sales and lost it back to the county for nonpayment of taxes during the depression. New York did not repeal the statute, as Professor Powell suggested in 1938. But his conclusion that there were no improvements that could breathe life into the system seems to have brought an end to any further use of land registration in the state.

North Carolina

North Carolina enacted its Torrens law in 1913. The earlier studies indicate that its provisions were largely used in the coastal parts of the state, where timber companies used it to establish boundaries and to prevent the loss of title from adverse possession. There appears to be no other use of land registration in the state.

Ohio

As one of the first states to show an interest in Torrens, Ohio passed enabling legislation in 1896, only to have it ruled unconstitutional the following year. A subsequent state constitutional amendment led to a new statute in 1913. Perhaps because of the earlier difficulties, the new statute permitted the withdrawal of land from registration by the simple act of surrendering the certificate to the registrar.

Although Torrens systems were started in more than half of Ohio's eighty-eight counties, frequent use was attained only in the larger cities, for example, Cuyahoga (Cleveland), Hamilton (Cincinnati), and Summit (Akron) Counties. The pattern seems similar to that of Boston, Chicago, and the Twin Cities in that much of the land originally registered was in the form of large tracts being groomed for residential development. However, there does not appear to be any significant use of land registration in the Ohio cities after the depression. While the urban programs continue to remain in operation, the number of registered parcels appears to be decreasing because of the existence of the voluntary withdrawal provisions.

Oregon

Oregon's Torrens law, originally enacted in 1901, was amended in 1911 to allow withdrawal from registration. The earlier studies, together with some commentary in one court opinion, indicate that it was only slightly used in seven of thirty-four counties in the state. In the largest county—Multnomah (Portland)—most of the earlier registrations had been withdrawn by the 1960s. The statute was repealed in 1972.

Washington

The state of Washington authorized Torrens registration in 1907. The right to withdraw land from registration was added in 1917. As with the other states covered in this section, little registration was actually accomplished. The Powell study indicates that by 1937 no titles had been registered in twenty-one of thirty-nine counties. In the largest—King County (Seattle)—only slightly more than 200 registration decrees had been issued by 1937. Hearings conducted by the Federal Trade Commission in Seattle in the spring of 1977 contain testimony indicating that less than one percent of the land parcels in King County was registered and that there had been only one new registration in the preceding ten years.

Great Britain

Introduction and Summary

As stated earlier, we intentionally confined our examination of Torrens to the experiments within the United States. There is a considerable degree of experience with land registration in many other countries. However, it is clear from a general review of the available literature that no two foreign registration systems are exactly alike. A combination of differences in legal standards, in attitudes toward personal property rights, and in historical and cultural perspectives concerning land use and control makes it impossible to compare effectively the various systems in use today for the purpose of drawing conclusions with respect to land registration generally.

We did, however, make one exception in the case of Great Britain, which moved to a compulsory registration system for London in 1902 after forty years of flirtation with the Torrens concept. Other English-speaking jurisdictions, for example, Australia or the western Canadian provinces, implemented registration at a time when much of the land involved was undeveloped and owned by the government. In contrast, the British system was attempted on the basis of existing development and private ownership of land. Since Great Britain also moved to a nationwide compulsory system (in 1925) after many years of a voluntary approach, it was felt that some attention to the experience might be helpful to the American perspective.

Despite a common legal heritage, it turns out that British real-property law is considerably simpler than that of the American states. The customs and practices are still more different. Yet certain observations can be made to provide general guidance relevant to the British experience with Torrens:

1. While total closing costs for residential transfers in Great Britain are somewhat lower than those commonly experienced in the United States, the difference is entirely attributable to differences in brokerage fees (sales commissions). The title-related aspects of British closing costs (for search, examination, and conveyancing services) tend to run close to double those that commonly prevail in America;
2. There are no significant differences in British residential closing costs (or the title-related aspects thereof) between registered land and unregistered land;
3. After more than fifty years of experience (seventy-five years in the London area), the national compulsory registration program has registered only about 60 percent of the land parcels in the country. Much of this was achieved because of government sponsorship of massive rebuilding programs necessitated by destruction during World War II;
4. The current annual expense of the compulsory registration apparatus exceeds 24 million pounds (in excess of $40 million).

History and Background

Following the recommendation of a royal commission, a voluntary land-title-registration system was authorized by Parliament in the Land Transfer Act of 1862. In general, England had no experience with public deed-recording systems of the kind established in the American states in the seventeenth and eighteenth centuries. The owner or possessor of land kept the documents of entitlement himself and produced them for examination by a prospective transferee. A rigid landed aristocracy and a custom of perpetuation of ancestral land holdings through family descendants contributed to this practice of "private conveyancing." It is possible that the lack of any recording system was a motivating factor in the drive to secure a registration system. To this day, some of the English and Canadian literature uses the word *registration* to apply not to the Torrens approach of registering *titles* but to what Americans call *recordation*, that is, the placing on file of ownership and related records with a public office.

Several years' lack of success of the 1862 English registration system—attributed to the expense and delays of the registration procedure—resulted in a study by another royal commission, leading to legislative revisions in 1875. Continued disappointments led to yet another revision in 1897, authorizing the establishment of compulsory registration through the use of simplified administrative procedures for "possessory," as opposed to ownership, titles. Under this approach, legal documents providing the basis for possession (that is, deeds and long-term leases) were required to be "registered" (filed with the registrar) at transfer. Certain other interests arising subsequently were also required to be registered, but the government neither certified nor guaranteed the title or the right to possession.

In 1902 this compulsory feature for possessory titles was first applied to the City of London. Much opposition—chiefly from the legal profession—led to yet another royal commission in 1911, but little changed until 1925. In the interim, the compulsory London requirement, focusing on possessory titles only, had developed little more than a basic but incomplete recording system analogous to the tract indexes used today by some deed-recording offices in the United States.

The 1925 changes—manifested in a Law of Property Act, a Land Registration Act, and a Land Charges Act (which created a rudimentary recording system for mortgages)—amounted to more of a revolution in substantive real-property law than a change in the registration provisions. Many of the complexities in title concepts derived from feudal days, which continue to plague American real-property law today, were abolished. This apparently led to substantial changes in public attitudes concerning registration generally. It is reported that registration of "absolute" titles (that is, ownership as opposed to the limited "possessory" titles registered under the prior acts) increased rapidly after 1925, along with voluntary use of registration outside of the compulsory London area. Beginning in 1929, the compulsory feature—requiring registration of at least the possessory title at the time of each new transfer—was gradually extended beyond London by a process of adding a new geographic area every few years. However, it took more than thirty years before the extensions went well beyond the London metropolitan area. At present, the land registry is nearing the final stages in extending the compulsory requirement to the last remaining metropolitan districts in England and Wales.

Land registration in Great Britain is an entirely administrative process. The registry has broad discretionary powers, which are judicial in character. While registration actions are subject to judicial review, court action appears to be invoked rarely. However, the official certification of title is subject to several statutory exclusions, referred to as "overriding interests," which are similar to, but more extensive than, their American Torrens equivalents. In addition, the registry follows a "general boundaries" approach to parcel measurement. Unlike American jurisdictions, titles are registered pursuant to general boundary descriptions referenced to official maps prepared by the ordinance department of the national government. According to the literature, the specificity of boundary lines associated with American real-estate procedures is considered a matter for agreement "between gentlemen," to be resolved privately only.

Another important difference from American law involves the rarity of liens other than mortgages. For example, there is no provision in British law for a mechanic's or materialmen's lien. On the other hand, a series of planning acts, beginning with the Town and Country Act of 1946, invest complex land-use control powers in local district councils, which, while not reflected on the registration certificate, are considered sufficiently important to the use and value of land to be researched and examined at the time of transfer. A final point, which is important perhaps only to illustrate the significance of cultural differences and the difficulties of making comparisons between different countries, lies in the fact that the registration records in Great Britain are private, not accessible to the general public. Thus, a prospective purchaser must obtain the written authorization of the certificate owner to inspect the records or obtain a copy or official search of the land register.

The Current Operation

The land registry is under the direction of the chief land registrar, who reports directly to the Lord Chancellor. According to the registrar's annual report for the fiscal year ending March 31, 1976, the total staff of the registry consists of 4,787 persons located in a central headquarters and eleven district offices. In that year, the operating budget required the expenditure of 21.6 million pounds. Receipts totaled 18.5 million pounds, yielding a deficit of 3.1 million pounds, despite a provision in the 1925 law requiring the operation to be self-sustaining. This was the second consecutive year of substantial deficit operation, and the annual report indicates a need for an increase in fees to prevent future deficits.

In this 1975-1976 fiscal year, the number of total registered titles in the country exceeded 5 million. The exact number of possessory and absolute titles, respectively, is not stated. However, the five million figure represents an increase of approximately 1.5 million in the five years since the 1970-1971 annual report. This suggests that a high percentage, if not a majority, of the registrations are possessory only. That is, the British land registry is still not regularly certifying fee ownership titles in the manner of the American Torrens systems.

A substantial part of the increase in registrations in the last 5 years is attributable to a series of additions of new geographic areas subject to the compulsory provisions. Pursuant to these additions, the population covered by compulsory areas was increased from 22.6 to 31.7 million, the latter representing approximately two-thirds of the combined population of England and Wales.

The proportion of registered to unregistered titles is not known. The 1975-1976 report cited earlier estimates that approximately two-thirds of all land sales are lodged for registration. However, it is clear that the incidence of initial registration is almost entirely attributable to the compulsory feature. In the 1975-1976 fiscal year, 261, 542 applications for first registrations were received in compulsory areas, compared with 788 in noncompulsory areas. This ratio has held fairly constant for the last five years.

Some illustration of the magnitude of an operation with five million registered titles is apparent in the annual workload of the land registry. In addition to the approximately 262,000 applications for first registration reported above for the 1975-1976 year, the registry processed 1.7 million other "transactions" (transfers, mortgages, liens, etc.) related to registered parcels and performed another 1.7 million services (official copies, register searches, map searches, etc.). In this respect, the registry's business activity is similar to that of the American Torrens offices we visited, but with the offices of the chief examiner of titles and the registrar of titles combined in a single administrative operation.

Examination of the last five annual reports of the registry indicates that the subject matter of computerization of records has been extensively studied for several years. The conclusion of the registry is that the conversion of all files to computer-readable form is not economically feasible. However, the office is continuing to explore the feasibility of various piecemeal approaches.

Impact on Residential Closing Costs

There is currently in Great Britain a considerable furor over the amounts involved in residential closing costs. This has produced a sizable body of recent public literature—ranging from that of *WHICH?* (the British counterpart of the American *Consumer Reports*) to an inquiry by a Royal Commission on Legal Services. The brunt of the attack seems to be laid entirely on the professional body of solicitors (lawyers). On the surface, there may be some justification for the concern. Studies we examined indicated that the title-related aspects of closing costs (that is, for search, examination, and conveyancing services) run on the average between 1.5 to 2 percent of the purchase price. Brokerage (sales) commissions are in approximately the same range. In contrast, recent studies on American closing costs indicate that title-related costs run in the neighborhood of 1 percent of the purchase price, compared to 6 to 7 percent for brokerage commissions. Thus, while total residential closing costs generally appear lower in Great Britain than in the United States, the title-related costs are considerably higher.

A relevant fact that emerges from this current debate over British closing costs is that there is no differential in costs between registered and unregistered land. In fact, a registered transaction costs more because of the registry fees—approximately 35 pounds (around $70) for an average 14,000-pound home, nearly 100 pounds (about $200) for a 40,000-pound home (which is about average in the London area). Information supplied to the Royal Commission on Legal Services indicates that the time saving in the search and examination of registered property is in the neighborhood of thirty minutes. This is similar to the comparable information we obtained from lawyers practicing in the different Torrens jurisdictions in the United States.

Another fact uncovered in our research is that two major American title-insurance companies have entered the British market in the last few years. There are insufficient data to evaluate the import of this entry. However, the similarity to the American Torrens experience is not easily overlooked. Whatever value one might attach to the land-registration concept, the available evidence suggests that it produces little measurable benefit in the reduction of professional efforts and related costs connected with the assurances deemed necessary for title accuracy and completeness.

Computerization and Multipurpose Land Data Banks

Much of the current American literature concerning land record keeping is heavily concerned with the subject matter of automation of title records, principally through the use of electronic information-processing technology, and with the development of yet more complex multipurpose land-related information systems, sometimes referred to as *cadastres*. We examined the developments in this area to see if any additional insight might be gained on the land-registration issue. Unfortunately, the numbers of current automation applications are few, while the literature is vast and growing. If anything, we learned that there is much yet to learn.

On its face, the broader concept makes sense. There seems to be no reason why the capabilities of modern technologies should not be utilized for land-related information systems. However, it seems clear that, independent of abstract technical capacity, a state of the art has yet to emerge. There is a striking lack of definition or agreement concerning the applications to be achieved by the automation of land records, the benefits that will accrue, and the investment that is or will be required.

Automation of Land Records

It is commonly accepted that the conventional approaches to land record keeping are something less than efficient. Many record systems are geared to owners, as opposed to land involved, and indexed in terms of the individuals concerned. Ownership records, mortgages, other liens, and court judgments are indexed in this manner. Other land records are land-oriented and indexed by descriptors of the parcel in question. To make matters worse, the various pieces of information that may be relevant in any given inquiry are often located in different municipal offices—for example, ownership records with the recorder of deeds, legal judgments with the clerk of courts, current tax arrearages with the county treasurer. Further, important land-related standards evolving from zoning, building, and environmental controls are neither parcel-specific nor person-specific and are located in yet other offices.

The list can go on and on. The problem is easy to describe. To many writers, the answer is so simple as to be misleading—the computer. Yet the reality is not yet here. We were able to identify a considerable number of specific automated applications for land-related information around the country. However, the experience so far appears to be heavily confined to such limited-purpose functions as revenue-gathering activities. There are numerous instances of computer use for property appraisal, tax assessment, and taxpayer billing. On a considerably lesser scale, there are also isolated examples of automated land-related information systems for special assessments (for example, for lighting and sewer improvements), for water and sewer services, for fire prevention and control, and for other municipal purposes.

In the context of title records, there are also a myriad of instances of limited-purpose applications. Many of these are in private plants operated by title companies. In the public arena, there appear to be several instances of semiautomated tract indexes. Typically, these indexes are accessed by a parcel descriptor and show a chain of title by ownership over a period of time. They do not generally contain other information that pertains to title status or otherwise relates to the land involved. There is only one current example in the United States of an attempt to integrate a wide variety of land-related information in a single data information system—that which went into operation in 1977 in Forsythe County (Winston-Salem), North Carolina.

The Forsythe County Land Records Information System (FCLRIS) is multipurpose, since it is designed initially to store information relevant for tax purposes as well as for title status. Information presently entered in the system is reported to include:

1. The chain of ownership back to January 1, 1944;
2. Some encumbrances, including current mortgages;
3. Appraisal and assessment information;
4. Current status for taxes and special assessments;
5. Zoning status; and
6. Boundary coordinates.

The FCLRIS system is designed so that it can be accessed by several different parcel descriptors: by a unique identifier; by street address; by deed book and page; by tax block and lot; and by name of current owner. A special feature is the assignment and use of unique coded identifiers for each land parcel. Constructed from modern surveying and aerial photo-mapping techniques, the identifiers are assigned consistent with established state and federal plane geodetic coordinates. It is thought that the establishment of this system of unique identifiers provides the base from which a seemingly infinite variety of land-related information can be entered and stored.

Since FCLRIS only recently began operation, there are no data available on actual experience, problems encountered, user benefits, and so forth. It seems clear that the system currently lacks all the information relevant to full title status. Court judgments, certain other liens, and easements are not currently entered into the computer-sorted information files. Thus, the system as currently planned offers something more than a computerized tract index but considerably less than information provided in a standard abstract of title. This raises some questions in our minds about the potential of the system to produce a meaningful reduction in the efforts and expense associated with title search and examination.

It is reported that the Forsythe system was built by a private contractor for the sum of $1.5 million. This contract was let after four years of planning, and the price quoted does not include public staff efforts involved in the planning, data assembling, and entry process. Thus, we estimate that the full start-up cost of this limited land-information system is in the neighborhood of $2.5 to $3 million. Since it covers approximately 144,000 land parcels, the unit construction cost is in the neighborhood of $17 to $21 per parcel, or approximately $11 to $13 per person, based on a county population of 230,000. These costs are within the range of estimates provided by recent studies undertaken to evaluate the feasibility of comparable systems by Fairfax County, Virginia, and in Massachusetts by a statewide land records commission.

Because of the unavailability of data on operating costs, on prior cost considerations, on the possibilities for new revenue-gathering services, and the like, we are unable to evaluate the cost-effectiveness of a system such as FCLRIS. It may be that the efficiencies in information retrieval generate savings in operational costs that justify the initial investment. Or it may be that additional applications may be required before cost-justification can be reached. Since FCLRIS is literally *the* pioneer in this area, it should be carefully studied and evaluated as experience unfolds.

This question of evaluation raises further questions concerning the criteria to be applied in evaluation. It is not clear, for example, that a reduction in residential closing costs via an improvement in title-search methodology is an expected outcome of the FCLRIS project. Seemingly, a properly developed system of the type described should produce a higher degree of accuracy than a manual search-and-retrieval system. It also seems that inquiries should be retrieved far more rapidly. The combination of increased accuracy and reduced search time could conceivably result in some reduction of the costs associated with title search and examination. On the other hand, it is possible that the justification of the investment involved lies with improvements in other

information applications or with the production of new information capabilities that were impossible to achieve without the computerized data base.

The Cadastre

The increasing interest in recent years in the development and automation of
land data information systems has been accompanied by the importation of a
French term—the *cadastre*. A cadastre is simply defined as a systematized
record of interests in a specific land parcel serving as a land tenure information
system. As such, it is nothing more than a multipurpose land-related information system, of which the FCLRIS project is a mini-version. Historically, the
concept of the cadastre is generally considered to have originated with the
reforms instituted under the regime of Napoleon. Its initial purposes seem to
have been to identify and establish control over land in the departments of
France that were remote from Paris.

In modern usage, the cadastre appears to be an accepted part of local
governmental programs in much of Europe. There is a considerable variety
of purposes for which cadastres are used, depending on local needs. In general,
it can be said that they are heavily associated with land-use planning and control.
Some common uses appear to be for soil classification, cultivation practices,
zoning, utility lines, building permits and code enforcement, public way and
easement rights, and, more recently, flood plain, wetland, and other environmental classifications. Police, fire, and other public protection agencies are
also users of cadastre information.

The current interest in the cadastre approach is a function of the availability of technological improvements—in information storage and retrieval
capability and in mapping and boundary-line identification techniques—and
of increasing demands for more and better quality information in every aspect
of social and economic life. Land ownership information, for the purpose of
tax assessment and collection, as well as for establishing title history, is one
of many functions handled by the cadastre.

In this connection, it is important to note that the cadastre concept is
separate and apart from the legal approach followed for the validation of title
status. Many of the European cadastres are associated with land-registration
systems that are not unlike our Torrens systems. Some, as in the case of the
FCLRIS project, are not. In fact, North Carolina is one of the few states with
a surviving Torrens statutory authorization. Yet Forsythe County chose to
implement its computer project without a land-registration component.

A sizable cadastre program is currently under development under the joint
sponsorship of the three maritime provinces of Canada (New Brunswick, Nova
Scotia, and Prince Edward Island). The available literature on the project suggests that it is well under way on a twenty-year program estimated to cost in

the neighborhood of \$21 million for the introduction and maintenance of the cadastre survey base (land parcel mapping identification) alone. Another \$50 million over the same twenty years is estimated for the design, implementation, and maintenance of land-registration and other information services contemplated. No information is available on the projected cost of the registration feature alone. The three maritime provinces are the only Canadian provinces lacking a land-registration system. Thus, the experiences encountered as the project unfolds will be highly relevant to some of the questions addressed here.

It is essential to conclude this brief discussion of automation by repeating our warning concerning the confusion in the literature between improving recording techniques and the merits of registration. These are separate and distinct issues that require independent evaluation.

Annotated Bibliography

The literature on Torrens is of voluminous proportions and, for the most part, is to be found in legal periodicals. Publications relative to the experience in the United States are reported here in three distinct time periods: early, middle, and current. Materials consulted on land registration in Great Britain are included, but we do not list numerous articles available on Torrens in other English-speaking jurisdictions or in other nations with a different legal heritage. Finally, we list publications (mostly of recent vintage) consulted on land-title problems generally, on automation of land-records systems, and on multipurpose land data systems.

Torrens in the United States: The Early Period (1890-1925)

The publications listed are of value because of the insights afforded into the historical conditions that contributed to the early legislative enactments and the tenor of the intellectual debate over Torrens that raged over three decades.

Balch, F.V. "Land Registration—A Different Point of View," 6 *Harv. L. Rev.* 410 (1893).

Beale, J.H. "Registration of Title to Land," 6 *Harv. L. Rev.* 369 (1893).

Brewster, J.H. "The 'Torrens Acts'—Some Comparisons," 1 *Mich. L. Rev.* 444 (1903).

Carret, J.R. "Reply to Criticisms of Land Registration," 7 *Harv. L. Rev.* 24 (1893).

Chaplin, H.W. "Suggestions as to the Question of Constitutionality of Land Registration," 4 *Harv. L. Rev.* 280 (1891).

_____. "Record Title to Land," 6 *Harv. L. Rev.* 302 (1893).

Crowley, J.H. "The Torrens System," 6 *Marq. L. Rev.* 114 (1922).

Kenny, J. "The True Way to Simplify Our Land Titles," unpublished (1906).

Hassam, J.T. "Land Transfer Reform," 4 *Harv. L. Rev.* 271 (1891).

Hogg, J.E. "Registration of Title to Land," 28 *Yale L. J.* 51 (1918).

Jones, L.A. "Land Registration," 32 *Am. L. Rev.* 760 (1898).

_____. "Land Title Registration in the U.S.," 36 *Am. L. Rev.* 321 (1902).

Kidd, A.M. "The Applicability of the Torrens Act in California," 7 *Calif. L. Rev.* 75 (1919).

Niblack, W.C. *Analysis of the Torrens System* (1903).

_____. "Pivotal Points in the Torrens System," 24 *Yale L. J.* 274 (1915)

Reeves, A.G. "Progress in Land Title Transfers; the New Registration Law of New York," 8 *Col. L. Rev.* 438 (1908).

Rood, J.R. "Registration of Land Titles," 12 *Mich. L. Rev.* 379 (1974).

Van Doren, D.H. "The Torrens System of Land Registration," 17 *Col. L. Rev.* 354 (1917).

Anonymous. "Land Title Registration in California," 41 *Am. L. Rev.* 432 (1907).

Anonymous. "Torrens States and Record," 16 *Law & Banking* 37 (1923). This is one of the first articles to report data on the actual Torrens experience in many states and is cited by many other writers. Unfortunately, we were unable to locate a copy.

Torrens in the United States: The Middle Period (1925-1945)

Publications in this period are largely dominated by the accumulated experience with Torrens, which showed many failures and substantial lack of use. Many of the articles show the influence of a comprehensive federal survey (WPA Project No. 6101) of the experience in each state by 1936. Unfortunately, we were not able to locate a copy of this study.

Bordwell, P. "Registration of Title to Land," 12 *Iowa L. Rev.* 114 (1927).

Cushman, E.H. "Torrens Titles and Title Insurance," 85 *U. Pa. L. Rev.* 589 (1937).

Fairchild, W. "Various Aspects of Compulsory Land Title Registration," 15 *N.Y.U. L. Q.* 545 (1938).

_____ . "A Criticism of Professor Richard R. Powell's Book entitled *Registration of Title to Land in the State of New York*," 24 *Corn. L. Q.* 557 (1939).

Henshaw, S.K. "The Torrens System in Ohio," 1 *U. Cinn. L. Rev.* 472 (1927).

Landels, E. A Review of the Torrens Experiment in the United States (1938). This unpublished study is one of many during this period that attempted to survey the entire American experience. Mr. Landels, a practicing attorney in San Francisco, was not in favor of Torrens.

McCall, F.B. "The Torrens System—After Thirty-Five Years," 10 *N. Car. L. Rev.* 329 (1932). This is another attempt to survey the American experience with Torrens. Professor McCall was a strong Torrens advocate.

McDougal, M.S. "Land Title Transfer: A Regression," 48 *Yale L. J.* 1125 (1939).

_____ . "Title Registration and Land Law Reform; A Reply," 8 *U. Chi. L. Rev.* 63 (1940).

Morris, P.C. "Land System of Hawaii," 21 *A.B.A. J.* 649 (1935).

Patton, R.G. "The Torrens System of Land Title Registration," 19 *Minn. L. Rev.* 519 (1935). This is a thorough analysis of the Torrens approach. Mr. Patton played a major role in the development of the Hennepin County system.

Powell, R.R.B. *Registration of the Title to Land in the State of New York* (1938). This is the most comprehensive of the Torrens studies and the more objective of those performed during this period. The study generated the criticism in the Fairchild and McDougal articles cited.

Sabel, S.L. "Suggestions for Enacting the Torrens Act," 13 *N.Y.U. L. Q. Rev.* 244 (1936).

Tanner, F.C. *Registration of Title to Real Estate* (1935).

Anonymous. "Survey of the Colorado Torrens Act," 5 *R. Mt. L. Rev.* 149 (1933).

Torrens in the United States: The Current Period (1945 to date)

The publications in this section include materials on the major existing Torrens systems. Articles marked with an asterisk (*) represent the work of the modern Torrens advocates.

Bennyhoff, C. Registrar of Titles Procedures (Hennepin County Registrar of Titles, 1967).

California State Lands Commission. *Report on Land-Title Law of the State of California* (1953). This comprehensive study led to the repeal of Torrens in California.

Farrell, E. "Introduction to the Concepts, Purposes and Scope of the Torrens System"; Sigford, M. "Procedure in Initial Registration & Proceedings in Hennepin County"; Peterson, E. "Original Land Title Registration Proceedings in Ramsey County"; Carroll, J. "Matters Affecting Land After Registration of Title, Including Proceedings Subsequent to Registration"; all in *Third Annual Real Estate Law Forum,* Minnesota Real Estate Practice Manual 15 (University of Minnesota, 1967).

Feinstein, F. "The Torrens System," in *Basic Real Estate Practice* (Illinois Institute of Continuing Legal Education, 1976).

Fiflis, T.J. "Land Transfer Improvement: The Basic Facts and Two Hypotheses for Reform," 38 *U. Colo. L. Rev.* 431 (1966).*

Heinrich, E.L. "The Case for Land Registration," 6 *Merc. L. Rev.* 320 (1955).

Hudak, L.M. "Registration of Land Titles Act: The Ohio Torrens Law," 20 *Clev. St. L. Rev.* 617 (1971).

Janczyk, J.T. "An Economic Analysis of the Land Title Systems for Transferring Real Property," 6 *J. Leg. Studies* 213 (1977). This is the only attempt to analyze Torrens quantitatively. It draws on Cook County data, but suffers from fatal misconceptions concerning the operation of Torrens.

Laugessen, R.W. "Torrens Title System in Colorado," 39 *Dicta* 40 (1962).

Lobel, M. "A Proposal for a Title Registration System for Reality," 11 *U. Rich. L. Rev.* 501 (1977).*

Maher, J.C. "Registered Lands Revisited," 8 *W. Res. L. Rev.* 162 (1957).

Maloney, J., and Thayer, H. "Land Court Practice and Procedure," in *Essential Real Estate Practice and Procedure* (Massachusetts Continuing Legal Education, 1976).

Patton, R.G., and Patton, C.G. "Registration of Titles and Conveyancing Applied to Registered Titles" (reprinted in Minnesota Statutes Annotated, Chapter 508).

Quinn, J.J. "Registration of Title: A Statutory Comparison," 4 *St. Louis U. L. J.* 229 (1957).

Whitman, D.A. "Optimizing Land Title Assurance Systems," 52 *G. Wash. L. Rev.* 40 (1973).*

Anonymous. "Torrens System in Illinois," 45 *Ill. L. Rev.* 500 (1950).

Anonymous. "Yes Virginia, There is a Torrens Act," 9 *U. Rich. L. Rev.* 301 (1975).*

"An Act Concerning Land Titles," Illinois Revised Statutes, Chapter 30, Section 45 *et seq.* (Illinois Laws, 1897, May 1, 1897, Section 1 *et seq.*, as amended).

"An Act Providing for the Torrens System of Registering Land Titles," Minnesota Statutes Annotated, Section 508.01 *et seq.* (Minnesota Laws, Chapter 237, Section 1 *et seq.*, as amended).

"The Land Court and Registration of Title to Land," Massachusetts General Laws, Chapter 185, Section 1 *et seq.* (Massachusetts Statutes, 1898, Chapter 562, as amended).

Transcript, Housing and Real Estate Conference jointly sponsored by the Seattle, Washington, office of the Federal Trade Commission and the City of Seattle Department of Licenses and Consumer Affairs (1977), pp. 230-429. This conference covered the cost of conveyancing and included discussion of the Torrens system in the state of Washington and in British Columbia.

The Experience in Great Britain

Chavasse. "Conveyancing and Other Non-Contentious Costs," *Oyez Practice Notes No. 20* (6th ed., 1975).

Crane, F.R. "The Law of Real Property in England and the United States: Some Comparisons," 36 *Ind. L. J.* 283 (1961).

Dowson, E., and Shephard, V.L.O. *Land Registration* (2d ed., 1956).

Fiflis, T.J. "English Registered Conveyancing: A Study in Effective Land Transfer," 59 *NW. U. L. Rev.* 468 (1964).

H. M. Land Registry. "Registration of Title to Land" (1971); "Report to the Lord Chancellor on H. M. Land Registry, 1971-72" (1972); "Report to the Lord Chancellor on H. M. Land Registry, 1971-73" (1973); "Report to the

Lord Chancellor on H. M. Land Registry, 1973-74" (1974); "Report to the Lord Chancellor on H. M. Land Registry, 1974-75" (1975); "Report to the Lord Chancellor on H. M. Land Registry, 1975-76" (1976).

Payne, J.C. "American Title Insurance in an English Context," 40 *Conv. & Prop. Law.* 11 (1976).

Rudinger, E. (ed.). *The Legal Side of Buying a House* (1975 reprint). This is a publication of the Consumers' Association in Great Britain.

Ruoff, T.B., and Roper, R.B. *The Law and Practice of Registered Conveyancing* (1973).

Simes, L.H. "Important Differences Between American and English Property Law," 27 *Temp. L. Q.* 45 (1953).

Simpson, S.R. *Land Law and Registration* (1976).

Anonymous. "The British Empire," a supplement in Powell, *Registration of the Title to Land in the State of New York* (1938) (p. 269).

Anonymous. "Conveyancing Fees and Charges," (Oyez Publishing Co., 3d ed., 1976).

Anonymous. *Registered Land Practice Notes* (The Law Society, 1972). This pamphlet was prepared jointly by the Law Society (the association of solicitors in Great Britain) and H. M. Land Registry.

Anonymous. "Is Your Solicitor Really Necessary?" *The Economist* (March 19, 1977) p. 24.

Land Registration Act, 1925 (15 & 16 Geo. 5, Ch. 21).

Related Materials

Barnett, W.E. "Marketable Title Acts—Panacea or Pandemonium," 53 *Corn. L. Rev.* 45 (1967).

Bayse, P.E. "Trends and Progress—The Marketable Title Acts," 47 *Iowa L. Rev.* 26 (1962).

_____ . "Modernizing Our Conveyancing System By Legislation," 31 *Tenn. L. Rev.* 176 (1964).

_____ . "A Uniform Land Parcel Identifier—Its Potential for All Our Land Records," 22 *Am. U. L. Rev.* 251 (1973).

Burke, B., Jr. "Conveyancing in the National Capital Region: Local Reform with Nation Implications," 22 *Am. U. L. Rev.* 527 (1973).

Cook, R.N. "American Land Law Reform: Modernization of Recording Statutes," 13 *W. Res. L. Rev.* 639 (1962).

_____ . "Land Law Reform: A Modern Computerized System of Land Records," 38 *U. Cinn. L. Rev.* 385 (1969).

Cretney, S. "Land Law and Conveyancing Reforms," 6 *Real Prop. Prob & Tr. J.* 108 (1971).

Cross, H.M. "Weakness of the Present Recording System," 47 *Iowa L. Rev.* 245 (1962).

Jensen, J.E. "Computerization of Land Records by the Title Industry," 22 *Am. U. L. Rev.* 393 (1973).

Leary, F., Jr. "Twentieth Century Real Estate Business and Eighteenth Century Recording," 22 *Am. U. L. Rev.* 275 (1973).

Lerner, H. *Feasibility of Computerized Land Title Search in Fairfax County* (1975). An analysis of the cost and impacts of a computerized land-title system for Fairfax County, Virginia; prepared by the Office of Research and Statistics at the request of the County Board of Supervisors.

Maggs, P.B. "Automation of the Land Title System," 22 *Am. U. L. Rev.* 369 (1973).

McLaughlin, J. "The Nature, Function and Design Concepts of Multi-Purpose Cadastres" (University of Wisconsin, 1972). This doctoral thesis provides a comprehensive analysis of the cadastre in a setting of modern technology.

Payne, J.C. "The Crisis in Conveyancing," 19 *Mo. L. Rev.* 214 (1954).

_____. "In Search of Title," 14 *Ala. L. Rev.* 11; 278 (1961-62).

_____. "101 Home Buyers: The Consumer, The Conveyancing Process, and Some Questions of Professional Conduct," 16 *Ala. L. Rev.* 275 (1964).

Plotkin, I.H. *On The Theory and Practice of Rate Review and Profit Measurement in Title Insurance* (1978).

Roberts, W.F. "Use of the Legal Cadastre in the Maritime Provinces of Canada," 5 *Rutg. J. Comp & Law* 121 (1975).

U.S. Departments of Agriculture and Commerce. *Land Recording in the United States: A Statistical Summary* (1974). This government study surveys the procedures utilized in land records keeping and storage.

U.S. Departments of Housing and Urban Development and Veteran's Administration. *Report on Mortgage Settlement Costs* (1972). Printed in Hearings on H. R. 13,337 before the Subcommittee on Housing of the House Committee on Banking and Currency; 92d Congress, 2d Session (1972).

Whitman, "Home Transfer Costs: An Economic and Legal Analysis," 62 *Geo. L. J.* 1311 (1974).

Massachusetts Land Records Commission Program Statement (1976). This report provides the basis for the Commission's recommendations for an integrated land data system and a work program for its demonstration.

Significant Reform and Modernization of Local Record Keeping of Land Title Information (1976). This is a "white paper" submitted to the U.S. Department of Housing and Urban Development by the Committee on Improvement and Modernization of Land Records, Real Property Division of the Real Property, Probate and Trust Section of the American Bar Association.

Symposium: "Computerization of Land Title Records," 43 *U. Cin. L. Rev.* 465 (1974).

Technical Bulletins No. 1-5, Forsythe County Land Records-Based Information

System (1975-1976). This is a series of bulletins describing the functions
and operations of the FCLRIS project in North Carolina.

The following are transcripts of recent conferences concerned with land data
systems. They contain many worthwhile articles and speeches on automation,
cadastres and multipurpose land data banks, and modern surveying capabilities:

Moyer and Fisher, *Land Parcel Identifiers for Information Systems* (1974). This
is an edited transcript of proceedings of a 1972 conference in Atlanta,
Georgia: Compatible Land Identifiers—the Problems, Prospects and Payoffs
(The CLIPPP Conference).
Proceedings of the American Congress on Surveying and Mapping (1977).
Proceedings of the Land Record Symposium (Orono, Maine, 1976).
*Proceedings of the North American Conference on Modernization of Land Data
Systems* (1975).

Index

About the Authors

Blair C. Shick is a senior consultant at Arthur D. Little, Inc., where he specializes in the distribution and regulation of consumer financial services. His recent work is in the feasibility and implementation of credit and check authorization, direct debit, and other electronic financial programs.

A graduate of Dickenson College and the University of Pennsylvania Law School, Mr. Shick is a member of the Consumer Advisory Council of the Board of Governors of the Federal Reserve System and has served as an adviser on the revision of the Uniform Consumer Credit Code to the National Conference of Commissioners on Uniform State Laws. He is currently a member of a committee that will recommend changes in the law required by the use of electronic funds transfer.

Irving H. Plotkin, senior economist and director of Arthur D. Little's Regulation and Economics Unit, specializes in forensic economics and in analyses of the effects of various types of government regulation, self-regulation, and taxation on industry capital flows, risk-taking, competition, and efficiency. His work in the fields of finance, industrial and welfare economics, and econometrics has included studies of the risk/return pattern in the American economy; studies in the field of antitrust economics (one involving the often conflicting objectives of free competition and efficient production for the Atomic Energy Commission and the Department of Justice, others relating to antitrust issues in the marine transportation, insurance, frozen food, drug, securities, real estate, sporting goods, and pet food industries); studies deriving economic interpretation of the Internal Revenue Code; and five major studies of prices, profits, and regulation in the property and liability, land title, and mortgage insurance industries, the results of which have been widely incorporated into state and federal insurance regulations.

Dr. Plotkin has presented the results of these studies before several U.S. Senate committees, the Federal Reserve System, the Interstate Commerce Commission, the Federal Maritime Commission, the Federal Trade Commission, the U.S. Court of Claims, U.S. District Courts, and numerous state legislative committees and regulatory agencies.

He has also served as a consultant to the Department of Justice (Anti-trust and Tax Divisions), the Atomic Energy Commission, the Federal Deposit Insurance Corporation, the Department of Housing and Urban Development, the Department of Transportation, the Department of Health, Education and Welfare, the Environmental Protection Agency, the Federal Deposit Insurance Corporation, the Federal National Mortgage Association, the Federal Home Loan Mortgage Corporation, as well as numerous industrial corporations and trade associations.

Dr. Plotkin received the B.S. in economics from the Wharton School (University of Pennsylvania) and the Ph.D. in mathematical economics from the Massachusetts Institute of Technology, where he taught computer science and finance. He has published more than 50 monographs, reports, and papers and has made more than 30 appearances as an expert witness before federal and state judicial, legislative, and regulatory bodies.